THEA WOOD

KICK FEAR IN THE FACE

EVERYTHING YOU WANT IS ON
THE OTHER SIDE OF FEAR

KIND WORDS FOR
KICK FEAR IN THE FACE

This book is a must read! The raw authenticity is captivating; but even more, it gives everyone hope that they can make an unbelievable comeback and turn their testimony into the very thing that makes them courageous through Jesus' strength. The practical approach and the bite-size applications make a comeback story possible for everyone. Thank you for this inspiring book!

Angel Barnett
CEO & Chair of Dream Institute/Short Creek Dream Center

During these volatile times, the book Kick Fear in the Face *is a game changer for us all! This book will not only inspire you, but challenge you. And it will give you the tools to rise to that challenge. Thea so beautifully shares her times of weakness and triumph. She is willing to put it all on the line so we can grow and learn as well. I've had the amazing opportunity to experience part of this journey with her, and one thing I know is that she doesn't just talk the talk, she also walks the walk. I hope you grab a notebook and probably some Kleenex, because, if you are like me, you will be wrecked (in a good way) by the words on these pages.*

Sumer Morenz
Original Fear Kicker

If you need someone to be your biggest fan, but unafraid to call you out, Thea is your girl. This book feels like a coffee date with a friend, a session with a coach, and a chance to start again. What are you waiting for? Dive in!

Megan Valentine
Founder of Team Brave & Author of *No Place Like Known*

Thea Wood is a close friend, hype woman, dream chaser, and world changer. I deeply respect and admire the way she lives her life to the fullest. If you're ready to kick fear in the face, she's your girl!

Havilah Cunnington
Fellow Fear Kicker & Founder of Truth to Table

Kick Fear in the Face *is a story of how Fear Kicker Thea Wood found strength in God throughout life's most challenging moments. Her story shows people, young and old, that with a little trust in God and the refusal to give in to fear, you can overcome anything! Thea is a strong voice that carries bold wisdom for the next generation amidst a culture that tells people to give in to life's challenging moments. If you want to get out of the cave that you are currently living in and learn to see the beauty of life around you, read this amazing book.*

Aubrey Matthesius
Women's Ministry Director at Dream City Church

Thea's journey is so inspiring! I'm thankful she recognized that fear is a dream killer and how she pushed through pain to create a life of abundance. I highly recommend her book, and her life story, to any and all who would dare to move beyond what is comfortable into the greatness that God has for those who believe!

Sheri Silk
Co-Founder of Loving on Purpose

THIS is a powerful book. Thea shares a journey of challenges and encouragement, of hope and authenticity, and of practical next steps to live life to the fullest. At every turn, her heart for Jesus will touch yours in the best, most life-giving way.

Jen & Marcus Jones
Creators of Leading a Significant Life Podcast

Get ready! Thea shares, out loud, her life experience with fear and drama. She outlines their crippling ways and shares effective tools and proven guidelines to starve them out of your life. Then with deep sincerity and great care, she draws you out of your comfort zone to find your anthem, draw a line in the sand, and become an observer of your own life to think, act, and believe the way you decide. Thea pulls no punches to tell you change is painful but so worth the generational fruit it bears. It's your Victor's Crown.

Chris Ziegler
Spiritual Mama & Prayer Warrior

The number one barrier to success in life is fear, and in this book you will recognize the breakthrough you need to help you take life-changing action and experience massive success! I have known Thea Wood since she was a teenager. She has always lived her life on mission and totally understands how to unlock mission in others. This is a must read for everyone who wants to live a life of MORE! This book is as practical as it is transformational. Everything that she wrote in this book she has lived every day for years. And because of this she has led thousands of people into transformational living. I really believe nothing great happens without dreams. But once you dream, you must have a guide! This book will truly give you everything you want on the other side of fear! It's a roadmap to reaching the destination God planned for you.

Pastor Lloyd Zeigler
CEO of Masters Commission International Network (1988–2019)

Step into your power and your best future today by following Thea's captivating and raw journey to breakthrough! You were made to be a contender and way-maker for yourself and the generations to come. Follow the path of Thea's captivating, anointed and raw story in Kick Fear in the Face *and watch your own future transform. Thea reveals the secret to her success to show you that you can do everything she has done. She was placed on this earth to be a light-bringer and world-changer, and you are, too!*

Pastor Ashli & Pastor Rowdy Van Horn
Pastors of One Church Scottsdale

Kick Fear in the Face...*I can still remember the first time I heard Thea utter those words. A powerful statement that needed to be shouted from the rooftops. The only thing more powerful has been watching Thea become the embodiment of those words. As a reader, you now have a front row seat to her transparent and transformational journey with step-by-step guidance from one who has actually walked it. You will now have this wisdom to take on your unique journey.* Kick Fear in the Face *is so much more than a statement; it's a way of living!*

Dave Blanchard
CEO of the Og Group & Author of *Today I Begin a New Life*

DEDICATION

To Amaya, Katelyn, and Phoenix:

As a girl my dream was to be a mama. You have made that dream come true! You are my heartbeat, and I wrote this book for you.

In these pages I share some of the darkest, most painful moments of my life. I want you to know what living your God-given destiny will really take. Rising to meet God's call on your lives will take grit. You will have to contend against an enemy that wants to take you down and stand up to a culture that wants you to compromise truth.

However, I also want you to know your power. You have the Spirit of the Living God inside of you. The unlimited source of creativity, power, and peace has made His home in your hearts! Jesus won the battle at Calvary—so live in that abundant life!

This book is also the story of how your family has contended to give you the life you have. We've laid a foundation for you to build on. Now stand on our shoulders. When life gets hard, when bad days string themselves together, don't stay down. Your job is to keep rising up, showing up, and never giving up!

TO DOUG, MY LOVER BOY!

This book is also a love letter to you.

I wouldn't be who I am today without you. Your partnership in all things is sacred to me. Without you standing beside me, we could have never created this crazy, beautiful, miraculously integrated life we have together. You are the fiercest Fear Kicker I know, and your encouragement means everything. Together we will change the world, our children, and generations to come will stand on our shoulders! They will know God and make Him known to the ends of the earth.

With passionate and relentless love,

Thea
(AKA, your Lover Girl)

CONTENTS

A NOTE FROM DOUG

My friends,

You know who a person really is by how they act when no one else is around. Well, I have been given a front row seat to who Thea is, often when she has no clue I'm around. She doesn't live her life behind a social media filter. She is 100 percent real, raw, and authentic.

You are about to go on a journey with a woman who has chosen to live apart from a noisy, distracting world. She seeks God in the secret place. Her ability to feel the weight of the world means that I often find her doubled over in empathetic pain, praying and crying out for someone else's healing or breakthrough.

Kick Fear in the Face was born in the refiner's fire. Since she was a young girl, Thea has embraced obstacles, believing they exist to make her better. She has lived differently, knowing her calling means walking the path less taken. She has navigated the deconstruction and reconstruction of her faith, embraced fear head-on, and learned how to become a praying wife (in what began as a non-praying marriage) when her husband was emotionally and sexually checked out. Thea has learned how to do hard things. She doesn't chase the easy life—she chases one of impact.

Above all else, she has a unique ability to authentically love people and meet them where they are at. And that's what kicking fear in the face is really about: love. I believe this book will guide you to do the same and even change the course of your life if you apply the hard-won lessons she shares in these pages.

Once you see something, you can never unsee it. So I'll even say, "Read this at your own risk!" You're going to uncover some things going on deep within your soul. There is no going back. But the best news is, she will help you blaze your own trail forward.

You'll find keys to unlock doors where you've been stuck. You'll find motivation to get back up and dust yourself off one more time. Most of all, I believe the lifestyle of kicking fear in the face will bring endless breakthroughs, helping you thrive in the areas that are most important to you.

Thea, you've created a masterpiece for generations to come!

Doug Wood

FOREWORD

What an honor to write about our friend and mentor, Thea Wood. In 2010, God brought us together in a simple yet supernatural way. We built a new home around the corner from Doug and Thea, and they ended up attending our church. At the beginning, Thea entered our life in real and practical ways. She created trust and equity in our relationship through time, consistency, and showing up!

Thea doesn't just write about practical ways of building authentic relationships; she did the work for years that now gives her the credibility to show others the way. She didn't have an agenda, but she was intentional about investing in our family. Over the last decade she has consistently modeled Christ-centered, people-focused love!

About seven or eight years ago, we had the privilege of watching Thea literally launch the "Kick Fear in the Face" movement as she proclaimed the breakthrough phrase, "It's time to KICK FEAR in the FACE!" and then did a jumping kick off of the stage at a coaching event. She shocked and inspired all of us with that bold move. What started as a call to action has turned into a movement and a mandate! We didn't know much of her story early on, but we have had a front row seat to the transformation of this radical influencer. We are constantly inspired by the Thea who is "fully awake to my purpose as a chainbreaker, way-maker, and light-bringer!"

In this book, Thea paints a vivid picture of the grip that fear can hold on us if we allow it. She validates pain with empathy, but at the same time, she emboldens us to take back the spaces of our lives that fear tries to own and actually become stronger as we break through and break free! Thea isn't just giving advice; she is leading herself first. And in the process, she invites us all to walk out our God-given purpose. From her practical advice about "getting really good at being in a room with just a few people" to reminding us that "fear leaves its residue on us," you will be awakened, confronted, and challenged to proclaim and live out your God-given potential. She refuses to play small and invites others to make that same commitment.

Here's the bottom line: we have been directly mentored by Thea (and Doug) for over ten years, and they have become some of our best friends. They model abundance to us in an attractive and inspirational way. The principles that Thea outlines in this book are many of the same principles that allowed us to go from surviving to thriving in every area of our lives. An abundance mindset and the courage to kick fear in the face gave us the audacious courage to pack up our family and belongings in 2016 and move to a community full of sunshine to design the best life possible for our family. The best part is the principles that Thea shares in this book help anyone who trades in their fear for bold action. This creates ripples, waves actually, of positive influence helping us do our part to make this world a better place.

Kevin & Bekah Tinter
Uncommon Freedom

PASTOR'S BLESSING

YOU' VE GOT IT!

I will never forget the words that I spoke over both Doug and Thea Wood around the year 2000. They were small group leaders, among other small group leaders, navigating a series most appropriately entitled *If You Want To Walk On Water, You've Got To Get Out Of The Boat* by John Ortberg. I was serving as a pastor in the Portland, Oregon area. I knew it then. I know it now. They walked in a special, unique leadership. They were Water-Walkers!

The Lord graciously allowed me to see just a portion of their gifting future: He would flow through them to indelibly influence the countless people; and, thank Him, they got out of the boat!

Thea Wood was an early Water-Walker. She craved more, not just a "good life", but a great life. She knew this only came from life in Christ Jesus, in a relationship, not a religion.

As a Water-Walker, Thea is sacred. She is a romantic toward her husband, her family, her friends, and especially to her Savior. She is sacred to her calling to be a chain-breaker, a way-maker, light-bringer, and to kick fear in the face!

We, as a pastoral couple, have been blessed to know Thea and her family for well over thirty years. We were there for the near tragedy of the touch-and-go with baby Amaya Rose in her beginning hours. We were called in the wee hours of the morning to come to St. Vincent Hospital and pray, and we witnessed a literal miracle! We have observed the high honor of dedicating the precious Wood children: Amaya, Katelyn, and Phoenix. These were all Water-Walking moments!

Throughout our pastoring-personal journey with this family, one of the constants has been Thea's R.E.A.L. Spirit. Believe me, Thea is REAL. What you see, is what you get. And we love it!

Thea is…

RELEVANT: One who is relevant is connected to the matter-at-hand. This is Thea! Whether it's a heart-to-heart talk with a dear friend, someone she has just met (she has never met a stranger!), her children, Doug (her "lover boy"), she is connected, she is relevant. She is especially connected to the Kingdom of God! You will discover this immediately in Chapter One of this incredible book you are holding! This book is relevant because Thea's heart is relevant.

ETERNAL: Thea's perspective always holds eternity in full view and vision. Her eyes are continually set on eternity- things that are everlasting, permanent, timeless. Our Thea lives not just for the now but for eternity. Thus, in this book, she shares the eternal liberty awaiting just beyond fear.

ACCEPTING: One of Thea's strongest, most admirable traits is her genuine acceptance of people. She holds no one "at bay." With wisdom, she opens her arms, her heart, and her "no-judgment-zone" mentality- all wrapped in Christ's love. Is Thea perfect? Nope! None of us are. That's the point of this book, for you are invited to journey the freedom path that

Thea has navigated and to receive your freedom on the other side of fear! Thus, this book comes from a spirit of honesty and humility, revealing to you the acceptance that Christ offered YOU! TODAY! NOW! You can walk triumphantly!

LOYAL: Thea holds faithfully to her commitments. She has an iron-clad devotion to fidelity and faith. She displays a spirit of honor, integrity, reliability, and sincerity. We have observed this over decades; she's never changed, only grown! It's not surprising that her favorite flower is a sunflower! How incredibly poignant, for it richly symbolizes adoration, loyalty, longevity, the sun itself! It is known as the "happy flower"! It is known as the perfect flower to brighten someone's mood. Now isn't all that Thea? I submit to you: these are all attributes of loyalty worked out, released in someone's life. We have observed and experienced these as true with Thea. And if you've met Thea, I am confident these have happened for you.

As a result, this book that you are holding, when engaged, will release a contending for freedom, true happiness, genuine joy, and the liberty of making the correct, healthy decision to be released from the enemie's snare of captivity called fear.

So what are you waiting for? Get out of the boat. Dive in and be a Water-Walker!

Kicking Fear in the Face with you!

Pastor Greg and Roxanne Hickman
Valor Family Pastor / Doug & Thea Wood's Personal Assistant

JESUS:
OUR
REDEEMER

Jeremiah 1:5

"Before I formed you in the womb I knew you,
before you were born I set you apart; I appointed
you as a prophet to the nations."

CHAPTER 1

OWN YOUR STORY

It was 10 p.m. on a Wednesday night in the mid-1990s. I trudged through the Iowa snow with a group of five high school girls, walking in circle after circle around our school building, praying for spiritual revival.

The icy wind may have made our faces numb, but the fire in our spirits kept us marching! Even in the winter cold, we circled that building like it was the city of Jericho*, just waiting for those spiritual walls to come tumbling down.

This was a typical weeknight for high-school Thea. Now, I wasn't completely awkward; I stayed active by cheerleading, being on the dance team, in drama club, and spring track. I wasn't popular, but I didn't go to public school to be popular . . . I wanted to make an impact for Jesus. During the day, I walked from class to class in a *Jesus Freak* T-shirt with verses on the back, carrying my Bible. I was fearless and unapologetic about living my faith out loud.

During this time, revivals were breaking out all over the United States and the world. So on the weekends, my parents took friends and me to these services, and sometimes my little sisters would tag along. I'd never experienced anything quite like it. God's presence was so real; it seemed like I could reach out and touch it.

We spent so many hours in prayer

* JOSHUA 6:1-27

and worship that it felt like we had jumped into the deep end of a pool. Then we went back to the normal world soaking wet. And a lot like a girl who walked around school with soaking wet clothes, I was teased for living my faith so openly.

I was different. But I'd been this way for as long as I could remember. God radically invaded my parents' lives when they were twenty-five. They immediately stopped drinking and cussing and began working on their marriage. They were totally devoted to Jesus and to each other. All I knew growing up was the foundation of faith they set in our home.

They committed to be at church whenever the doors were open, which meant two to three times a week. They joined a community group from church, and those families became fast friends.

I encountered the love of God by asking Jesus into my heart at just five years old on a tree stump in the middle of our family farm. Honestly, I don't remember a day not serving the Lord since then.

My childhood was filled with Dr. Charles Dobson sermons, Focus on the Family studies, and visiting places like Whit's End from an old-school Christian audio drama called *Adventures in Odyssey*!

My parents' commitment to Jesus changed everything. They broke the hold of alcoholism on our family. They kicked nicotine addiction to the curb. They put an end to the affairs and promiscuity that had been so common in our family bloodline.

Both of my grandfathers came out of serving in World War II with deep-seated anger issues they didn't know how to deal with. These had trickled into my family line like toxic chemicals silently leaking into a river system. It was because of my praying grandmothers, Edith and Lavanna, that over time my grandfathers, Martin and Ralph, accepted Christ; and the bitterness, anger, and toxicity started getting washed away. While it left its residue on my parents, they contended against those generational beasts well.

They broke real chains that had held my family back for generations. And when you break chains, you break them forward and backward.

I encountered the love of God by asking Jesus into my heart at just five years old on a tree stump in the middle of our family farm.

MARTIN & LAVANNA FREY

RALPH MANN, KNOWN AS A GREAT HORSEMAN

It impacted my grandparents, my siblings and me, and now all our children.

Faith transformed my family. And because of my parents' unwavering walk with Jesus, being ridiculed in school for my faith and commitment to purity didn't bother me up to this point. I just kept being me . . . Thea, the farm girl who loves Jesus and reads books like *I Kissed Dating Goodbye*.

Then my junior year of high school happened.

There was a guy I'd grown up with who I really liked, but he only liked me on and off. I never dated him because he didn't take his relationship with God seriously. He'd date other girls, cross lines I was unwilling to cross, and then come back to me. I held the line and stayed true to my convictions, but that's when I paid a price.

A group of girls (some Christians, others not) painted a big L on my locker and told everyone I was a lesbian because I was saving sex for my future spouse. This hurt. It was confusing and embarrassing. And even though I'd been so solid, I wavered bit by bit. The tiniest cracks started forming in my faith foundation. Standing up for Jesus made me weary, and I stopped shining brightly.

Toward the end of that school year, I went to Germany as part of a student exchange program. This is where everything unraveled.

THE WOMEN WHO CAME BEFORE ME

It is often said that the first sound we hear in the womb is our mother's heartbeat. Actually the first sound to vibrate our newly developed hearing apparatus is the pulse of our mother's blood through her veins and arteries. We vibrate to that primordial rhythm even before we have ears to hear. Before we were conceived, we exsisted in part as an egg in our mother's ovary. All the eggs a woman will ever carry form in her ovaries while she is a four-month-old fetus in the womb of her mother. This means our cellular life as an egg begins in the womb of our grandmother. Each of us spent five months in our granmother's womb and she in turn formed within the womb of her grandmother. We vibrate to the rhythms of our mother's blood before she herself is born...

LAYNE REDMOND,
WHEN THE DRUMMERS WERE WOMEN

GRANDPARENTS
MARTIN & LAVANNA

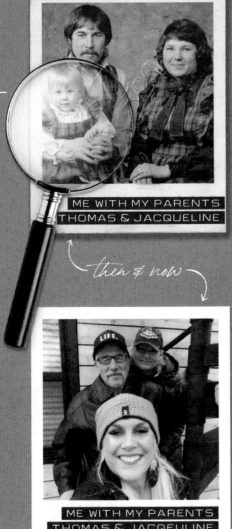

ME WITH MY PARENTS
THOMAS & JACQUELINE

then & now

ME WITH MY PARENTS
THOMAS & JACQEULINE

My Wishes For You

These are my wishes for you That you apply the
Christian principles taught you all
through your life. The Lord is available
to help at all times. He touches lives
in a special way. What a Wonderful World
this is! Look around-there is beauty
every where—We can help preserve all
of these wonders by doing our part & help
others in seeing it too. Our out look on
life can help others.
    Most of all I ask the "Lord" to keep
you & "Doug" in "His" care.

GRANDPARENTS
EDITH & RALPH
PRAYER ABOVE FROM EDITH

GREAT-GRANDPARENTS
DELLA & WILL

GREAT-GRANDPARENTS
ELMA & CHARLES

2ND-GREAT-GRANDPARENTS
KATHERINE & CHRISTIAN

THE RESTING PLACE OF MY
4TH-GREAT-GRANDMOTHER,
ANNA KERSTEN MOSEBACH,
IN THE PIONEER CEMETERY IN
KEYSTONE, IOWA

3RD-GREAT-GRANDMOTHER
MARTHA MOSEBACH

MY FAMILY LINE

THEA (MANN) WOOD

PARENTS
JACQUELINE (FREY)

PARENTS
THOMAS MANN

GRANDPARENTS
LAVANNA (KNIPP)
& MARTIN FREY

GRANDPARENTS
EDITH (CONKLIN)
& RALPH MANN

GREAT-GRANDPARENTS
ELMA (GOKEN)
& CHARLES KNIPP

GREAT-GRANDPARENTS
DELLA (FARR)
& WILL CONKLIN

2ND-GREAT-GRANDPARENTS
KATHRINE (STRUBE)
& CHRISTIAN GOKEN

2ND-GREAT-GRANDPARENTS
ANNE BIRGITHE LUDVIGSDATTER
MADSEN VIE & REUBEN A FARR

3RD-GREAT-GRANDPARENTS
MARTHA (MOSEBACH)
& ANDREW STRUBE

3RD-GREAT-GRANDPARENTS
INGER JOHANNE MOSESDATTER
ULLBUST &LUDVIG MADSEN
ULLEBUST

4TH-GREAT-GRANDPARENTS
ANNA (KERSTEN)
& CHRISTIAN MOSEBACH

4TH-GREAT-GRANDPARENTS
BRITA TRONE MADSDATTER
ALBOST (ULLEBUST) & MOSES
OLSEN

5TH-GREAT-GRANDPARENTS
CATHARINA M. GUNTHER
& HARTMAN KERSTEN I

5TH-GREAT-GRANDPARENTS
HELENA JOHANNESDATTER
HESTAD & MADS ANDERSEN
INDREBOE

HOW DID I GET HERE?

Have you ever found yourself in a place where you just know you shouldn't be? Where you realize, okay, I definitely don't belong here. Maybe you're making some decisions you never thought you'd make. Or you're making compromises in areas where you swore you'd never give in. In Germany, I found myself doing *all of the above.*

The drinking age there was fifteen. So one night, I followed some of my new friends into a grungy basement club. We walked right into the middle of a rave. Yes—glow sticks, rivers of alcohol, and people doing things I'd never seen in Iowa. Alarm bells went off, telling me to abandon ship, but I didn't listen.

Music pumped so loud I could feel it in my chest. We had to yell just to hear each other. The atmosphere was totally out of control. Then my new German friends started doing shots.

A little voice of reason whispered, "Thea, what are you doing here?!"

I ignored it. Then I took my first shot . . . and second . . . and third . . .

Suddenly the Jesus Freak girl from Iowa was getting drunk in a German club. And thousands of miles away from home, my decisions got even worse. I left the rave in a car with one of the guys we'd just been drinking with.

He sped off through the city. We kept going faster and faster, even into the countryside where sharp curves came out of nowhere. The tires screeched and he weaved from one side of the road to the other. He was laughing; I was gripping my seatbelt so hard my knuckles turned white.

With my heart pounding louder than the music in that club and the taste of cheap alcohol still on my breath, I prayed. "God, if you save me from this, I will not allow this to be my story!"

Thankfully, He did.

"God if you save me from this, I will not allow this to be my story!"

We made it back to my host's house and I finished out my time there, keeping far away from clubs, alcohol, and reckless boys in cars. But still, that moment stayed with me. When I got home, I knew it was time to make good on the commitment I'd made to God about the story my life would tell. I was struggling, and even though I didn't dare tell my parents about what I'd done, they could tell I needed something different.

So that summer in 1997, between my junior and senior years of high school, my parents let me spend the summer in Colorado Springs, Colorado with my Uncle Ern and Aunt Moni. I literally flew from Germany to Chicago to Denver, not even stopping to see my family. My parents knew I was struggling in my faith and wanted me to spend time with my aunt and uncle, who were my childhood pastors. And once I got to Colorado Springs I attended a revival called Prayer Storm '97. Afterward, I stayed with my Aunt Moni and Uncle Ern for a fun summer filled with church, small groups, drinking coffee, and hanging out at Whit's End at Focus on the Family. I'm grateful my parents didn't hold on so tightly to me that they slowed God's growth in me. They gave me the perfect amount of space and freedom in the right place.

These were pre-cellphone days. So instead of text messages, my mom and I sent a journal back and forth. I'd write a few pages to her, and she'd write a few pages back. Every week we did this.

One of my entries stands out to me (see next page).

PAIN AND PURPOSE

That summer changed the course of my life. I knew Germany Thea was not who I truly was. After going back to school, I kept proving that to myself throughout the year and into the next big stage of my life. But as I look back on that time, I see more clearly what had happened.

I started losing who I truly was when I listened to the voice of fear.

Thank-you so much for letting
me come here this summer!
It has truely blessed me and
I matured spiritley, I don't think
pshicially though (but that's O.K.)
Anyway, GOD IS SO AWESOME!
It had to have been in his
plan, because everything AWESOME
and in step!! I got to be a
part of teens that love the
LORD with a passion, and
take that and make it
mine also! GOD is SO GOOD!
He is such a WORTHY 3
HONORABLE GOD!! Thanks Mom
for your love for GOD and
me!!
        Signing Off for my
    first summer away from
    Home! Love You so
          much!

"What will people think if I keep doing this Jesus thing . . . ?" I was worried.

Fear began controlling my thoughts, actions, and identity. It took me years of looping through these cycles of fear and doubt to understand that everything I truly wanted was on the other side of fear. And that meant being the version of Thea who was fully awake to my purpose as a chain-breaker, way-maker, and light-bringer!

Kick Fear in the Face is a message, mission, and movement about going on the attack against fear. It's about contending for who you were made to be and living that purpose out loud.

God has used the hardest moments in my life as seeds. And those seeds have blossomed into trees of purpose.

He turned my pain points into purpose points through continual surrender. Surrender to say, "God I don't understand. I'm afraid. But I'll follow your voice anyway."

The Lord has done so many amazing things in my life through these moments. He's always revealed the action steps one by one.

After Germany, I spent the rest of my time in high school reclaiming the spiritual ground I felt I'd lost. By the time I graduated, my spirit

If you want to go fast, go alone. If you want to go far, you need a team.
-John Wooden

MASTERS COMMISSION FRIENDS WITH OUR FAMILY
ANGEL BISHOP, TRAMMEL ORR, JUNIOR SILIGIA, AMAYA WOOD, DOUGLAS WOOD, KATELYN WOOD, SHAY GALLOWAY, AND ROHMON MERCHANT.

was fully prepared for what was next: Masters Commission in Phoenix, Arizona.

Masters is a program where students completely devote themselves to God. Almost like someone turned Bible college into a bootcamp for Jesus. It's about figuring out your purpose and becoming everything God made you to be. Our days were filled with intense discipleship training, worship, prayer, and real-life ministry. We traveled the country, sharing about Jesus in churches, school auditoriums, and every place in between.

This is where I met my husband, Doug. He is the absolute love of my life and partner in all things. We fell in love over that year and started dating once we left the program. Then things happened FAST.

We both wanted to give our relationship a real shot—marriage was on our minds. So, this little farm girl from Iowa moved across the country to Oregon, where Doug was from. I moved in with his grandma while we figured each other out and then planned our wedding.

It all seemed so perfect. Like our lives were moving in the right direction. We were both on fire for God and thought we'd go into ministry, like all our friends graduating Masters Commission were doing.

We got married, but all too soon, the honeymoon faded. Life hit us hard, and our first few years of marriage were rough.

My old insecurities bubbled up. I was in a bad place physically, overweight and self-conscious. I didn't want to admit it, but I saw the truth behind some of my high school zeal. I didn't stay committed to not dating purely out of love for God. The real roots, insecurity about my weight, ran deep.

I was terrified of what people would think about me if I risked vulnerability. I had an unspoken belief that allowing myself to be known would mean rejection. And these old fears crept into my heart like weeds, choking out my spiritual health.

That's what unchallenged fear does: it kills the best of what's inside of you. It's an enemy that strangles your potential. It steals away your future by keeping you paralyzed.

Unchallenged fear kills the best of what's inside of you.

YOU'LL ALWAYS BE . . .

In Russia, there's a plant called hogweed that's so poisonous its sap causes blindness and third-degree burns. It grows six feet tall and has leaves as big as umbrellas. It's so toxic that it kills everything around it and grows especially fast in neglected soil, completely taking over entire fields.

I've seen fear do the same thing in my life and the lives of so many others! The places of past pain that we try so hard to avoid get taken over. Its toxic sap burns and hurts and scars us. So we stay as far away as possible.

Just like this crazy Russian plant, the longer we let fear grow, the harder it is to take back ground.

But my fellow Fear Kicker, I'm here to tell you that these territories can be taken back. Fear can be chopped down. Soil can be revitalized. And beautiful things can grow again.

It's possible. It just isn't easy.

The toxic fear weed took a deeper root in Doug's and my first years of marriage. Not only did I have personal insecurities, but the future we'd imagined was slipping away.

I was going back to Masters Commission—but Doug and I decided if we were going to work, I needed to move to Oregon. Doug felt like he was called into business with his dad. So, our decision really became ministry or business? Our path was business.

I moved to Oregon. Doug's future was clear. But what about mine? Why would God take me through this intense discipleship training of Masters Commission only to slam the doors of ministry shut? But that was exactly what happened.

Suddenly, I wasn't the girl who was going to change the world and pack stadiums for Jesus. I was going to be a businessman's wife. I felt like I had to let the most important part of myself die. Fear kept showing its fangs. Fear that I'd never become who God made me to be. Worry that it was my fault because I was letting my fire for Jesus die. Doubt that I could be enough for the love of my life.

I felt like I'd lost myself. Have you ever felt like this?

It's like you look in the mirror and wonder,

"How did I get so far away from the person I dreamed of becoming?"

My heart cried out for a breakthrough in my marriage, health, finances, and spiritual life.

Inside I was yelling, "Will the real Thea Wood please stand up?!"

Doug and I both brought our own forms of dysfunction into our marriage. And we listened to what people said. "You'll always be . . ."

I gained weight and believed I'd always be that way because "you'll always be overweight, but it's okay to be unhealthy."

Debt piled up and we were told to get used to it because "you'll always be in debt; that's just how the furniture business is."

Our marriage crumbled and we heard our divorcing friends say, "You'll get divorced too because marriage isn't what any of us thought it was."

Their words were like a broken record stuck on repeat. And we listened. We believed. Addictions took their foothold. Stress was our constant mode.

However, there was one voice that we hadn't heard at first. It was quieter than the rest, almost like a voice coming from the back of a noisy theater. Finally, Doug and I listened to this voice—the Holy Spirit, our saving grace. The Spirit of the Living God awoke inside of us, reminding us of His promises to protect, His power to restore, and His love of providing.

What does that actually mean?

For me, it meant surrendering. I would fall to my knees on our white carpet at home and cry out to God. I was desperate for our marriage to change—most of all, I was desperate for Doug to change! I remember chucking a book I was reading across the room. It was The *Power of a Praying Wife* by Stormi Omartian. And I was outraged that she would tell me to pray for Doug when he was the one who was supposed to change! But what I didn't know was that Doug would fall to his knees on the red carpet in the back of our furniture store, crying his own tears, seeking God's voice in secret.

Now, God didn't wave a magic wand. Our lives weren't instantly fixed. But we kept trying.

I knew that if we were going to move forward, we had to become better versions of ourselves. I dragged Doug to every marriage retreat I could find. We jumped into every fad diet that came our way. We tried and failed . . . tried and failed.

Finally, after years of these cycles, I was about to turn thirty. That's a big number, and it made me reflect on my past and look ahead to our future. I was a momma, which made my heart so happy. And a wife to the man I loved, which I'd always wanted to be. But I knew it was time to surrender and try something totally different.

I had forty extra pounds of fluff, and Doug was sixty-five pounds overweight.

Facing thirty made me reflect on our past and look toward our future. Was this really going to be our story? Overweight, overworked, overtired, and just plain over it all?

I was able to take a hard look and know that if I kept doing what I was doing, I wasn't going to get any closer to my goals. This became another moment of surrender and filled me with urgency.

I had 40 extra pounds of fluff and Doug was 65 pounds overweight.

A SINGLE DECISION

For the first time in my life, I owned my story. I'd been trying to find

the way back to my fire and purpose for so long; it seemed like parts of me had died. But when I surrendered to what God had in store for us, I finally saw my places of pain as points of purpose.

For the first time, I clearly saw the generational crap that was trying to take us out, break apart our marriage, and steal our legacy.

Even in the journal entry I'd sent to my mom when I was in Colorado Springs, my health was totally incongruent with who God created me to be. This surrender moment happened in January 2011. In prayer, I saw this picture. Thousands of people were crowded together, stuck, held up by something. And I realized that something was ME!

I saw behind my eyes what God wanted to do through our hands. We were called to do amazing things, helping thousands of people get healthy in body, mind, spirit, finances, and relationships. But God wanted to do this in our lives first.

I tapped into a huge vision and made a decision, my lack of commitment wasn't going to hold anyone else up. Just like I'd circled my high school praying for revival, I saw that Jesus wanted to start the revival in our living room before taking it to anyone else's.

Our physical health had taken generations before us down. We'd made peace that it was just "in our genes." But this was it. Time to own that story and take back control.

Imagine ancient explorers landing on a beach thousands of miles from home. To keep themselves from leaving in fear or sailing away from discomfort, they burned their ships. No going back.

I burned the ships˙—the only option was to move forward.

A single decision changed our lives, and hundreds of thousands of others, forever.

As I write this, I'm so humbled by what God has done through not just my decision, but the thousands of other decisions it nudged in the right direction. Our physical health transformed from a place of pain and defeat into our place of power and victory.

SCAN ME

· WATCH AN AMAZING MUSIC VIDEO BY KING & COUNTRY CALLED BURN THE SHIPS

I lost those forty pounds, and Doug lost those sixty-five, forever. But we gained so much more. We identified that we were marked with a purpose beyond our own health. It was time for us to pay the gift of breakthrough forward.

It didn't all come with a tidy bow. It was messy for a while! But this is truly when we stepped off the hamster wheel and stopped playing around. We weren't going to look behind, to the right, or to the left. From there on, it was only forward.

We felt like pioneers trudging ahead, one step at a time. We had to figure out this new way of life and business as we went. The rest of this book is devoted to the lessons we've learned on that journey.

OWN YOUR STORY

One of the questions Doug and I get asked so often is how we've achieved the business and lifestyle we have today. I think the best way to share the journey as a whole are these two images.

SUCCESS

What people think it looks like

KICK FEAR

what it really looks like

Success isn't a straight line. It's a journey filled with hurt, pain, and hard decisions, where the victors are those who simply didn't give up.

If we think about your path to success like a hike, the trailhead is owning your story. It's the only place to start. Because when you own your story, you can find your voice, which is the honest expression of who you truly are. Owning your story is a place of full alignment, surrender, and impact. It's alignment with your inner self, surrender to God's purpose for you and impact, because you kick fear in the face and help others break free in the process.

Owning my personal story wasn't easy for me. The more people I've journeyed with, the more I've seen that it's hard for almost everyone. We all have our reasons for this, but mine was good ol'-fashioned fear. (What else is new?!)

You met crazy Jesus girl Thea at the beginning of this chapter. For years, it was hard for me to validate myself, to believe that my story actually mattered. After all, my dirtiest secret at that stage in life was getting tipsy in Germany. Compared to a lot of people, that was pretty tame! But do you see what I did there? I compared my story to other people's and had the false belief that my experience didn't count because it wasn't hard enough.

Let's call that out for what it is—a lie!

Today, I'm grateful that my parents laid a foundation of faith. Because my life didn't stay easy. In fact, it got really, really hard—especially in our first years of marriage. I'll share more about that later in this book. But for now, I want you to know that your journey to impact and kicking fear in the face starts with owning your story.

To own your story means turning your *pain points* into *purpose points*. It means not comparing your experience to anyone else's as more or less valuable. Guess what, my friend? You matter. Your story matters. You are made for wonderful things in this world. But there are two things you must understand:

Your purpose is unique to you.

Your purpose grows from the soil of past pain.

My pain was being ridiculed for my faith, feeling totally insecure about my body and physical health, and contending for a thriving marriage.

Today, do you know what I spend my life doing? Boldly sharing the hope I have in Jesus, helping others achieve optimal health and self-confidence, and investing in my marriage and family with Doug (my Lover Boy!). I find purpose in each of these because I struggled so deeply in these areas.

Once you accept your story and own it, you will find your voice.

FIND YOUR VOICE

Fear, the kind that shakes you from deep within your belly, entered my life when I was two years old. I was an adventurous farm girl, always running around our acres of property, climbing trees, hopping fences, and chasing animals. As the firstborn, I thought I was a superhero. I'd fall down and bounce right back up.

One day, I was doing the crazy thing two-year-olds do—leaping across furniture from chair to chair. I missed my landing, fell, and severely broke my leg. More pain than I'd ever experienced lit up my little body. I immediately cried and told my mom, "I'm not okay . . . I'm not okay . . . I'm not okay . . ."

 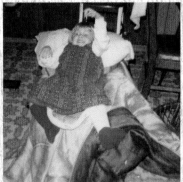 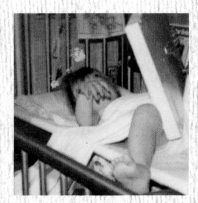

I was hospitalized and bedridden for forty days. Even though I was just two, I vividly recall this experience. And those words have echoed in my heart and head ever since: "I'm not okay . . . I'm not okay . . . I'm not okay . . ." From that point forward, my parents always worried about me. Fear and trepidation took root in my life.

When did fear enter your life? When is the moment you first remember being afraid—like the terrified kind of being scared?

This matters because like hogweed, that toxic fear grows and spreads. It holds our courage in its grip. I became too cautious and scared to take risks from that point on. It might seem like I'm making

THE
WHISPERS
OF
DOUBT
ARE
FEAR

a big deal out of something a lot of kids go through, but fear leaves its residue on us. And to break those chains requires us to see it, name it, and give it a face to kick.

That little girl inside of me needs to be told, "It's okay, Thea. God is partnering with you in this. It doesn't matter what other people think. There are too many lives at stake for you to play small."

On my journey, if I'm stuck and not experiencing a breakthrough in an area, I go back and ask, "Where is this coming from?" I trace it to the source. And every time I do, I find the face of fear. I hear the whispers of doubt for what they are: fear.

If you don't know, you stay stuck. But every time I've become aware of the fear holding me back, I've found massive victory in my health, marriage, business, and everywhere else that matters. And this is the process of finding your voice.

Who are you? Are you owning your identity? Are you expressing your unique gifts? Are you confident in your story and who you are made to be?

When I started Kick Fear in the Face, it was a moment where I felt like yelling, "Will the real Thea Wood please stand up?!"

My life stopped being about what I thought other people expected or approved. They weren't responsible for my destiny; I was! To do this, I've held on to Psalm 139:14 for years now: "I praise you because I am fearfully and wonderfully made; your works are wonderful, I know that full well."

You are on this earth for a purpose, and it is unique to you. You are a wonderful work of God's hand, His highest form of creation. My friend, it's time to reclaim who God created you to be. And that starts by seeing what story God wants to tell through your life. And news flash—it's probably not debt, bad health, fear, playing small, or crumbling relationships!

I remember a moment where God spoke to me. Some people hear from God like a distinct voice in their head or a gut-level knowing in their heart. I felt this distinct impression: "If you want to speak in front of thousands, you must learn to use your voice." I'd grown up seeing people like Billy Graham and Carman use their voice. In fact, I was in many of these stadiums, and I always knew I wanted to be part of that. But finding my voice didn't start on a stage. It started by getting really good at being in a room with just a few people.

After all, if I couldn't be vulnerable in that airplane seat with someone randomly put beside me, how could I ever expect to have the voice to share authentically with one hundred, one thousand, or ten thousand people? Finding your voice all starts with the one, not the many. And the power of your voice grows as you share with the one. Boldness, even when tiny, sparks a fire to speak out and testify.

How many people go to the grave without doing or saying the things they wished they had? Own your story and share authentically, speaking life instead of death. And even when that internal dialogue of doubt starts yelling you down, accusing,

"You're not enough . . . You're not a leader . . . Your story isn't special enough to help anyone . . ." you and I both respond this way:

"I am fearfully and wonderfully made."

I have a story to tell and a voice within me that matters. So do you! And a hurting world desperate for hope needs us to share it. This is how we thrive in this one life we've been given. Don't hold back! Own your story. Use your voice. Rise up to your destiny.

Understand that some people won't be ready to hear it. Be okay with that. Your story is not for everyone, so focus on the one who it is for. Because you can help the right person become exponentially more, and they can do the same for you.

Your voice is your power. God spoke the universe into existence; He spoke to dry bones and made them come alive, and He told a dead man named Lazarus to come forth (Genesis 1:3; Ezekiel 37:5; John 11:43)! Let him speak through you. You're not holding this book by accident. You're not settling for what life is throwing at you right now.

Your yes has incredible power to bring the abundance into reality. And now, it's time to:

OWN YOUR STORY.

FIND YOUR VOICE.

FOCUS ON THE ONE.

FORGET ABOUT THE MANY.

DO THE WORK.

STAY THE COURSE.

Let's change the world together!

Hebrews 10:24-25

"And let us consider how we may spur one another on toward love and good deeds, not giving up meeting together, as some are in the habit of doing, but encouraging one another—and all the more as you see the Day approaching."

CHAPTER 2

BUILD YOUR BEEHIVE COMMUNITY

Let's talk about bees.

Every week my son Phoenix and I look at a honeybee project at his school. They fly, buzz, and pollinate, doing all the things that bees do. As we've watched, we've also learned. What I find most interesting is that bees live in a colony.

Rather than thinking about a beehive as a little house where all the bees are roommates, you can better understand bees as a collective. A single organism made up of many black and yellow parts.

Every bee has a part to play.˙

SCAN ME

˙ LEARN MORE ABOUT THE MAGIC OF BEES HERE

We all know the queen. There's only ever one in each honeybee hive. She lives the longest and has the crazy task of laying tens of thousands of eggs and mating with other bees (while flying in the air). The vibe she puts out with her pheromones controls the mood of all the other bees. And she's the leader who helps the colony grow to as many as sixty thousand bees in a hive. Crazy!

Next there are drones. These are the boys responsible for helping the queen make bee babies. But sorry guys, they don't do much—and it's not very long until they're kicked out of the hive to fend for themselves!

Lastly, we have the worker bees. They're the ladies who act as nurses and cleaners, who warm and cool the hive, and more. Until finally, in the last ten days of life, they set off from the hive to forage. With about five hundred miles of strength in their wings, they waste no second to provide for the colony.

They are the real heroes of the hive. Without all the single ladies, nothing gets done!

The harmony of bees is magical. Because if any one of them would decide not to show up, the whole colony suffers. Their success is so intertwined, you can't separate them from one another.

In my life, I've had seasons where I'm hip to hip with a vibrant community of co-creators, where we're all on the same mission and level of intention. Few things are more powerful or fulfilling than this experience!

I've also had seasons where I felt like a lone worker bee, flying along, hoping for someone to journey with me. Or being surrounded by people who weren't the right tribe for me to fly with.

You know what the difference between these two communities is?

A beehive community shares drive, passion, and purpose, operating at the same frequency. You're only as strong as the people in your collective. Who you surround yourself with determines so much of what you can achieve. This won't be a comfortable crew to run with. They'll push you and call you up to greatness. They'll bring out the best in you.

A breakthrough doesn't happen in your comfort zone. While it won't be easy, I promise it will be worth it.

In this chapter, I want to encourage you to find your beehive community, to find your tribe and love them hard. And most importantly, I want to share how I've done it (and am still doing it) in my own life.

That last part was a mystery to me at times. I'd heard things like "you become the average of the five people you spend the most time with." And I longed for a community like this. But guess what? It never popped up on its own. It took action, intention, and most of all, a recognition that it was time to re-evaluate who I was surrounding myself with.

FIND YOUR TEAM BRAVE

Like bees, there's magic in finding where the people you want to run with spend their time. Where is the beehive? Early in our coaching career, Doug and I invested heavily into our personal development. We'd done this for years in our spiritual life, spending time at church every week, in small groups, Bible studies, conferences, marriage retreats, worship nights, and of course, Masters Commission.

We realized it was time to treat the other areas of our life in the same way. Massive growth and momentum happen in the right community. You're only as strong as the people you surround yourself with.

I had to take a hard look at my collective. I realized that to do the things I wanted to accomplish in the world, I had to put myself in environments where I was challenged. It was scary and so uncomfortable at times. But this posture of leaning into challenges helped me connect with the right people. I also got into the habit of saying yes to every chance to be around high-quality people—and what happened next was the perfect opportunity to keep flexing that muscle!

Doug and I were at a conference we went to every year, and I was invited to an early morning coffee with Megan Valentine. She asked me to arrive at 7 a.m., before the event started for the day because she had something to share with me. I didn't know Megan well at all, but I did know she had a reputation for achieving big goals and casting massive vision. So, I showed up.

Megan and her husband, Dan, were moving out of traditional ministry and into marketplace ministry. It was a massive move. So, what did she do? She asked seven ladies from across the country to come alongside her in this transition season. Every week, we'd meet on a video call and check in, stay accountable, and help each other.

This was a big thing to ask—and pretty gutsy. However, it just so happened to be the very thing I'd been craving and praying for. In doing this, she brought all our dreams together.

She called this first little group her Team Brave. Fast forward, and Team Brave is now a thriving community that's grown to over ten thousand women in pursuit of community, fulfilling their God-given purpose, and living their one and only life to the fullest! And it all started because Megan had felt like I did: super alone, isolated, and in need of a serious beehive community.

EARLY TEAM BRAVE MEETING

MEGAN AND I

SCAN ME

· **YOU CAN CONNECT WITH MEGAN AND TEAM BRAVE HERE**

Over the years, there have been different pockets of community like this, the right people with whom I chose to run at the right time. Now you might be thinking, "Oh, that's nice, Thea. I'm glad you had someone like Megan reach out to you. But no one's invited me to coffee to join a movement!"

Trust me. I get that. I understand what it's like to feel alone, unseen, and like no one is willing to include you. Being the odd woman out isn't a fun feeling. However, can I challenge you with some tough love I've needed to hear myself in different seasons?

Be a Megan! Kick fear in the face and step up, mommas and papas! Megan had the audacity and boldness to act. She felt the same way—which is why she sent those messages, made those calls, and, even though I'm sure she was nervous, did it afraid.

If no one's invited you, maybe it's because you're supposed to be the one doing the inviting!

This chapter is to encourage you and challenge you to ask, "Why not me? Why not create the beehive I want to do life with? Who's waiting for me to step out?"

You gotta be like a bee, stop worrying about the "me" and focus on the "we"!

There's incredible power to co-create in a collective. We can be like the honeybees, creating something more wonderful than we could ever imagine on our own.

MURMURATION

In 2018, energized by the power of community, I co-hosted a conference called Branded with Megan Valentine and another inspiring leader named Jen Jones. The theme meant that we were each branded with God's love and purpose. They were a unique mark on our lives. But the question was, would we realize it and rise to His call? Our tagline was "It's your time to fly!".

During this time, I was walking through significant postpartum depression. It was a dark season all around. Doug's parents were divorcing, and even though our business was thriving, I felt like

BRANDED CONFERENCE

important structures in our lives were falling apart.

So I held on tightly to Matthew 6:26, where Jesus said, "Look at the birds. They don't plant or harvest or store food in barns, for your heavenly Father feeds them. And aren't you far more valuable to him than they are?" (NLT).

I believed that if God took care of the birds, he would take care of us! So as I prepared my talk for our conference, I dove deep into birds. And I was quickly blown away—especially by starlings. Much like a beehive, I'd found another wonder of collaboration. In my research, I came across a YouTube video that still inspires me to this day.

Two girls are canoeing toward a small, tree-covered island on a loch in Scotland. You can hear their conversation and the lapping of the waves on the shoreline behind them. And then something dark appears in the distance—almost like a cloud made of black water. The cloud rushes toward them, moving low over the water, and then, without warning, soaring high into the air.

The cloud isn't really a cloud at all. It's a murmuration of starlings.

Murmuration is a phenomenon when thousands of starlings fly in unbelievably coordinated patterns. They resemble massive ocean waves crashing into each other and then scattering again and again. It's honestly one of the most beautiful things you'll ever see.˙

SCAN ME

˙ YOU CAN WATCH THE VIDEO WITH THE STARLINGS HERE

Their coordination seems impossible. How could thousands of birds move in artistic unison? Even in the wind and elements, they swoop in perfect formation, moving so fast you can hear the wind against their wings.

Of course, there's a scientific explanation. A study found that the starlings stay in formation not by paying attention to the whole, but by focusing on their nearest seven neighbors. And when they each keep wing to wing with their flying buddies, the entire community performs one of nature's most beautiful dances in the sky.˙˙ Not only is it breathtaking to watch, it serves them all. Murmuration deflects their enemies and even keeps them warm. It's a true wonder of the world.

SCAN ME

`·· ` **READ ABOUT THE SCIENCE OF MURMURATION HERE**

I shared about the magic of murmuration at the Branded conference. It was a powerful time! One of my favorite parts was when I shared the Time to Fly! Manifesto I'd written with my co-hosts. We all stood and declared it together!

Right now, wherever you're at, I want you to declare this manifesto out loud. Notice I didn't say "read;" I said "declare"! I want you to proclaim it and speak it out loud with the conviction that it's true. Its power lies in your belief. Go ahead and declare:

Time to fly manifesto

I belong to a family of brave,
fear-kicking people.

I am placed on earth for such a time as this!

I am purposefully designed;
I am called to nurture this generation
and fiercely love humanity.
I will fall more in love with my Creator
and Savior daily.

Today, I choose JOY!
Today, I choose HOPE!
Today, I choose LOVE!

I choose to live this day as if it were my last.
Spirit of God, shine bright through me.

Today is my TIME TO FLY!

IT'S TIME TO SHOW UP

So, how do you find your beehive community, your tribe, your murmuration? You just keep showing up. That's half the battle. Most people just don't freaking show up. For whatever reason, they stay home and play it safe. They don't buy that plane ticket to fly across the country. They don't attend that conference that God wants to use to rock their world. They don't make running with world changers a priority.

I promise you this is the main reason people stay stuck.

My goal has always been to put myself in the environment of the people I want to be like. So maybe right now, your step is simply to ask, "Outside of my spouse and children, who do I spend the most time with? And are they people I want to become more like or less like?"

Welcome to a hard conversation! But there is great power here, because you're searching for the authentic you. It's a mission to look at why you were created and then to assess if you're striving toward that goal, mark, and prize. And if not, getting into the right room with the right people is the fastest way to change your life.

WHAT ROOM ARE YOU IN?

A little over a year ago, I watched a video where Steven Furtick and T. D. Jakes were talking through some Bible stories in ways I'd never heard before. Pastor Steven gave Bishop Jakes a song title from the musical Hamilton, and then he would preach a one-minute sermon from it. It's amazing and you should watch the whole thing.

My favorite mini message was based on the song "The Room Where It Happened," and Bishop Jakes shares the story we often call "Doubting Thomas" in John 20:24–29.

> One of the twelve disciples, Thomas (nicknamed "the Twin"), was not with the others when Jesus came. They told him, "We have seen the Lord!"
>
> But he replied, "I won't believe it unless I see the nail wounds in his hands, put my fingers into them, and place my hand into the wound in his side."
>
> Eight days later the disciples were together again, and this time Thomas was with them. The doors were locked; but suddenly, as before, Jesus was standing among them. "Peace be with you," he said. Then he said to Thomas, "Put your finger here, and look at my hands. Put your hand into the wound in my side. Don't be faithless any longer. Believe!"
>
> "My Lord and my God!" Thomas exclaimed.
>
> Then Jesus told him, "You believe because you have seen me. Blessed are those who believe without seeing me."

Thomas joined the other disciples after they had seen Jesus risen from the dead. But he hadn't seen it and didn't believe them. For eight days the disciples talked about this, and for eight days Thomas thought they were crazy. Then they were together again in a room with the doors locked. No one could go out or come in.

Suddenly, Jesus!

He was spirit enough to pop into the room without opening the door but human enough for Thomas to touch His hands and side. At exactly that second, our Doubting Thomas was filled with faith—but only because he was in the right room with the right people.

Bishop Jakes said something amazing about this. "The power of being in the room will determine the destiny of his ministry and his life."

Christian tradition says Thomas traveled by sea to India, bringing the Gospel there. And he was so totally convinced that Jesus had risen from the dead and was God's son who died for the sins of the world, he was martyred for that cause. Amazing that Doubting Thomas became one of Jesus's most dedicated disciples.

All because he was in the right room!

FIND YOUR ROOM, MAKE YOUR ROOM

Some of us need to find the right room. We need to stretch ourselves and get uncomfortable. Because the right people in our lives—our beehive community living on fire for big dreams and impact—aren't going to be comfortable to be around. Don't get me wrong, the people in my room are amazing, positive, and life giving! But they love me too much to let me settle for less than I'm capable of. And I do the same for them.

Here's the truth, Fear Kicker: your room is where your breakthrough is. It's worth every ounce of effort to get into. Seriously, Doug and I have invested hundreds of thousands of dollars over the last ten years to step into the right rooms. I'm not asking anyone to make unrealistic or poor financial decisions. But if you want to advance forward in business, life, ministry, or any place else, I am challenging you to invest beyond what you ever have before. This means time, effort, money—and yes, leaning into discomfort!

If you don't get yourself into the right room, those dreams sitting inside you may never come into reality. In my dreams, I have stadiums filled with people to serve, every one of them ready to take massive action. So, I'm putting myself in the room with others who also want to fill stadiums. This benefits us all because they need help doing that, just like I do.

None of us can do God-sized things on our own. I'm texting, calling, and emailing people, asking, "How are we going to fill stadiums? In spite of COVID-19 and the way the world has changed, how will we impact thousands?"

Your beehive community is about both pursuing the room and creating the room. To rub shoulders and co-create with world changers, you might need to take the first step. And here's the deal with beehives: when they're thriving and growing, a group will separate from the hive to start a new colony. Sometimes it's time to leave and develop a healthy culture that you lead.

For the Wood Family, this looks like opening our home to youth. We're creating space for four boys whose mom is going through cancer. Right now, they're living on food stamps and really contending for health, structure, and their future. You know what they need? The right room!

Doug takes them out on Corvette rides and ATV rides in the desert, and he helps them see life outside of what they're going through. As young teenage boys, they're being thrown some curveballs. Our job is to be their beehive and show them abundance. We're showing them that there are people who authentically care about and love them.

Now, I don't share that to prop us up and tell you how great we are. I want you to see that creating the room other people need to be in is just as important as finding your own room. And Doug and I are far from the only ones doing this. We have so many business associates who are big thinkers focused on using their abundance to change lives.

Whether it's partnering to create pregnancy resource centers, adopting kids who desperately need a home, or simply fostering a loving atmosphere in your home, beehive communities are about life change! And when you get into the room with people committed to changing lives, you find inspiration and direction.

Doug and I are constantly humbled by the communities we get to do life with. When our family moved to Scottsdale, we didn't know a soul! Our son Phoenix wasn't even around yet—just Doug, me, Amaya, and Katelyn. But slowly, these beautiful, thriving communities have formed. They each started the same way: by getting us into the right room with the right people.

A FIRST-OF-ITS-KIND, GLOBALLY-MINDED COMMUNITY

Around ten years ago we met an entrepreneur named Angie Taylor who'd worked in traditional and private schools. She'd been a teacher and principal in multiple states and educational systems. However, she had big visions for what modern-day education could truly look like.

Why were our kids getting stuck in status quo, brick-and-mortar buildings? Why couldn't we use technology and globally-minded families to teach, reach, and change the world? About five years ago, we talked with Angie about what this could look like. Her dreams resonated with what Doug and I wanted for our kids. And after some praying and planning, we went all in together to co-found Valor Global Online, the first and only globally minded online learning community.·

SCAN ME

· LEARN MORE ABOUT VALOR GLOBAL ONLINE HERE

It's an all-virtual school with a rhythm of in-person retreats, connection, and travel to our global sister schools in Kenya, South Korea, the Philippines, Haiti, and Guatemala, with even more campuses being added. Because when a student enrolls in Valor, a child in a developing nation also receives an education because of our One2One global initiative!

Our kids aren't just learning in classrooms led by our world-class teachers; they're experiencing what it's like to help change someone else's life. Together, we created an innovative school that, little did we know, God had been positioning us for. And the incredible Valor Global Online community couldn't have started and matured at a better time.

When the pandemic took schools across the world virtual in 2020, we were there, ready and waiting to welcome hundreds more kids and expand our impact. It took a lot of kicking fear in the face to start Valor Global Online. But it has been so worth it.

Friends, I promise, your yes to step into the scary seasons, the risky opportunities, and the rooms filled with world changers will lead to massive breakthroughs. Yes, for you and your family. But also for dozens, hundreds, or even thousands of others!

Today, we're seeing massive fruit—but we had to put ourselves out there. We had to invest. We had to challenge our status quo. We had to disrupt our comfort zone. Together, we visualized the impact we wanted our brief time on earth to make. And even though we didn't know exactly how to do it, we identified who we needed to do it with. That's what it takes—doing that over and over again.

SCAN ME

˙ **FIND YOUR STRENGTHS!**

YOUR FUTURE IS BRIGHT

Getting into the right room will amplify your natural gifts and abilities. One of my favorite tests to find your superpowers is called CliftonStrengths. My number one strength is called Futuristic. For me, dreaming and vision casting are energy creators! It fills me with life to look ahead and imagine what's possible.

It also comes with this weird ability to clearly see the potential in others. This has served me well in business and ministry because I can sit down with someone and instantly see their potential—even when they can't see it in themselves. God has wired us all differently, and this just happens to be how he hooked up my wires!

Allow me to use my gift for a moment.

The fact that you're reading this book tells me something about you—especially that you're at the end of this special chapter. I believe you have what it takes to become everything you are meant to be. But I also know you will need people in your life who will draw your strengths out.

If you're ready to pursue the bright future of impact waiting for you, remember, it's on the other side of fear. It can be scary to reach out to people who you think may never even message you back! You might worry that people will think you're a fraud or imposter. That they may wonder, who does she think she is to have such big dreams? Or, why would he think he could possibly be so ambitious?

I'm here to tell you it's not what the doubters think—it's what dreamers do that makes all the difference. Find your beehive community today. Get ready to step into a room that will challenge you to level up and elevate yourself. You'll have to get gritty and endure resistance. You'll have some hard conversations because it's time to step out of some rooms you've stayed in for too long.

HERE'S THE KEY TO UNLOCK
THE DOOR TO ALMOST ANY ROOM:
BE HUMBLE, HUNGRY, AND SMART.

- The humble part comes by valuing what others have to teach you. This is coachability.
- The hungry part comes by connecting with your great purpose. This is hustle.
- The smart part comes by investing in yourself. This is personal growth.

Two rooms are waiting for you: the one that will elevate you, and the one that it's time to create. The right community will truly bless and empower you like nothing you've ever experienced. It is your rocket fuel. Now kick some freaking fear in the face, step into new rooms, and embrace getting uncomfortable.

It's time to fly!

SCAN ME

˙ MAKE THE TIME TO FLY MANIFESTO YOUR PHONE SCREENSAVER HERE

Spark Habits:
1: drink water
2: make your bed
3: put your armor on
4: get moving
5: sleep
6: prayer & meditation
7: get grounded

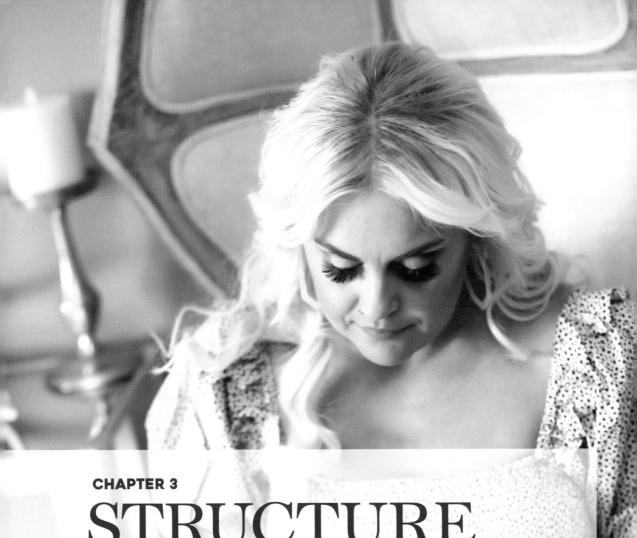

CHAPTER 3

STRUCTURE DETERMINES BEHAVIOR

I'm a free spirit. A go-with-the-flow girl. For the longest time, I wasn't interested in agendas or outlines, just in-the-moment decisions. I called myself "Spirit-led," meaning that I listened to the Holy Spirit's direction throughout the day. But the truth was that my resistance to structure wasn't creating health, happiness, or momentum in my life.

It was just the opposite. I flew like a kite in the wind, wondering why I never moved forward. I had still embraced small structures in my spiritual life of devotional time, prayer, worship, and church; but I kept them siloed.

Everything in me resisted structure and routine. To me, those words sucked all the fun and spontaneity out of life. I wasn't interested in living in a constrictive time prison. However, I was so wrong about what structure really means.

Today, I call myself a "free spirit embracing structure." Instead of keeping me chained to the ground, structure has helped me soar. I've seen it do the same for literally tens of thousands of people in the last decade.

No matter how you've felt about structure in the past, it's time to consider that embracing key routines, boundaries, and rhythms might be the missing ingredient to breakthrough success. The right structures are superpowers. They amplify your strength and keep your kryptonite at bay.

URGENT!

Structure helps you say your best "yes!" every day. But how many times do we put off the critical things? It's so easy to let the most important aspects of our lives slide.

Our personal health gets put on the backburner . . . Our spiritual life gets left on the shelf because of busyness . . . Our family time gets taken over by other priorities . . . And on it goes. If you're raising your hand and saying, "Whoa, Thea, this is me right now! The most important things in life are taking a backseat," then here's what I'll say: "You're not alone!"

This isn't a personality problem; it's a people problem—even the most disciplined humans struggle against structure at times. The only difference is, now that you've seen this in yourself, what are you going to do about it?

There's a really interesting concept that came from Dwight D. Eisenhower, the thirty-fourth President of the United States. Before he was president, he was a general in World War II. As so many soldiers did, he left the war with a deeper understanding of what was most important in life. He said, "What is important is seldom urgent, and what is urgent is seldom important."

He developed this idea into a simple grid called the Eisenhower Matrix.* It's a system for prioritizing how to spend your time, and it will serve us well as we learn to embrace structure! It puts our to-dos in four buckets:

SCAN ME

* **WATCH A VIDEO ABOUT THE MATRIX HERE**

1. Top left: important and urgent
2. Top right: important but not urgent
3. Bottom left: not important but urgent
4. Bottom right: not important and not urgent

The most important stuff in life is usually the stuff we find in the top right, important but not urgent. Exercise is important, right? But remember the last time you skipped your workout? You may have felt a little bad, but nothing terrible happened, did it? Nobody died! All that happened is you missed a session at your gym, on your bike, or on the trail.

	URGENT	NOT URGENT
IMPORTANT	1	2
NOT IMPORTANT	3	4

It isn't urgent, so the crazy things that pop up at work can quickly steal that morning me time. But over time, pushing off your development in key life areas becomes an issue. I saw this in my own life through weight gain, marriage struggles, money problems, spiritual stagnation, and so many other things. Like a garden with so much potential beauty, I was overrun with weeds instead of flowers.

Maybe you can relate?

Embracing structure is about making room for the important, but usually non-urgent things in our lives.

This is the place where our greatest fulfillment, impact, and purpose lies! If you want to change your behavior, start by setting a structure that serves you.

Fear Kicker, don't flirt with structure—marry it! Go all in. Sprint down the aisle and shout, "I do!"

In my experience, there are five structures that can radically change your life and your whole community's lives. My journey to fully embracing structure in my life started in the place where I'd been losing throughout my life . . .

EMBRACING PHYSICAL STRUCTURE

Growing up, I was a cheerleader—and anyone who's taken it seriously knows that cheerleading is a sport. You have to train hard and work on your conditioning, flexibility, strength, coordination, and nutrition. Movement was a part of my everyday life. But after graduating high school, I let it go to sleep.

Even though I was an athlete, I still had to fight being overweight. This problem had always nipped at my heels, and no matter what I did, I couldn't seem to shake it. After getting married and becoming a mom, my health got seriously out of control. I have already shared that I was forty pounds overweight—but what I didn't share are the details of how insecure that made me.

I was embarrassed about my body and struggled in intimacy with Doug. I constantly worried I wouldn't be enough for him. I was consumed by thoughts of what people must think about me. I hated the way clothes fit. Everything was either too tight or too baggy. And no matter what new diet or workout DVD I tried, I failed. Over and over and over again, I lost a few pounds, then gained even more back.

I was the yo-yo queen! But finally, I came to a place where the pain of staying the same was worse than the pain of change. It was time to get off the hamster wheel of diet, binge, shame, repeat.
Simply put, I had a broken physical structure. How did I fix it?

I discovered what I call my Spark Habits. They are things you may already do every day that you can level up to create massive momentum in your life. They are small but mighty. Anyone can do them and change their lives.

For me, it started with water of all things: the first Spark Habit.

SPARK HABIT #1: DRINK WATER

Water is nature's beauty juice! Drinking water was something I just didn't do, and that didn't seem like a big deal. But right when I actually gave my body the hydration it needed, my eyes opened. I learned that water is actually a workhorse in your body.

Here are just some of the jobs it does for us:

- carries nutrients and oxygen to our cells
- flushes bacteria from our bladders
- helps our digestion
- prevents constipation
- normalizes blood pressure
- stabilizes our heartbeat
- cushions our joints
- protects organs and tissues
- regulates body temperature
- maintains electrolyte balance*

Water keeps every system inside of us functioning the way it should! I took drinking eighty ounces as a challenge (my competitive nature always seems to kick in), and I believe this simple shift paved the way for my physical transformation. Let me challenge you to drink the appropriate amount of water for your body every day. Typically, it's at least sixty-four ounces, and often the right amount is up to half your bodyweight in ounces. I truly believe that if you can drink your water, you can change your health.

SCAN ME

* CLICK HERE TO READ, "HOW MUCH WATER SHOULD YOU DRINK?"
HARVARD HEALTH, 25 MAR. 2020

SPARK HABIT #2: MAKE YOUR BED

Navy Seal Admiral William H. McRaven said, "If you want to change the world, start off by making your bed."* If you make your bed, it's one thing you can come home to and already have accomplished. Life might be hell in a handbasket, but you've achieved at least one thing. And remember, it only takes a spark to light the world on fire!

SCAN ME

* WATCH HIS INCREDIBLE TALK HERE

SPARK HABIT #3: PUT YOUR ARMOR ON

Fashion is confidence. Putting on your daily armor connects your heart and your mind. It's taking command of your body. Your mind might be saying one thing, fear might be trying to shout you down, but you're there standing firm in your armor, ready to kick it in the face at every moment.

There's something about putting on your running shoes that motivates you to run. Putting on that baseball cap and showing up. There's a mind-body connection when you put on your clothing.

What you put on is how you choose to show up in the world. Shift out of the PJ mindset. You're no longer "just a mom" or "just a dad"—you're putting on your Wonder Woman or Superman cape ready to warrior up!

SPARK HABIT #4: GET MOVING

Y'all, exercise is about so much more than our waistlines! Some doctors even prescribe it to help treat conditions like anxiety and depression.* Yes, exercise is a drug—and a really good one you don't even need an insurance card for.

At first I had the idea of grinding out workouts alone in a gym where I felt totally awkward and out of place. There was a concept in my mind that exercise freaking sucked, but it was a necessary evil. But when I found my beehive community, my mindset completely shifted.

Community is everything for me. So instead of approaching workouts like a task list item, I looked for ways to be with people (especially outside, which we'll tackle next chapter). I found groups of amazing people to hike with. I signed up for 5Ks, then half-marathons, then even a full marathon! I dove into bootcamps and group fitness classes.

Combining structured workouts with community completely changed the game for me. Being with the right people in the right workout rooms constantly gave me the extra momentum to push through days where I didn't feel like eating right or training. That's the power of the beehive.

No matter where you are, just start. Take the stairs, sweat every day, get your good vibes (endorphins) flowing, take a walk to inspire creativity, park as far away as you can from the store or office, put on your gear right away in the morning and get yourself involved in a bootcamp or scheduled group fitness program. Even if you don't have anyone else right now, structure will be your workout buddy. Have a plan to spark transformation.

SCAN ME

* **READ MORE ABOUT EXERCISE'S POSITIVE IMPACT ON MENTAL HEALTH**

SPARK HABIT #5: SLEEP

Each night, rejuvenate, replenish, and optimize your emotional and physical health through quality sleep. Scientifically, lack of sleep creates cortisol and stress and makes it almost impossible to lose weight. According to the Johns Hopkins School of Medicine, sleep deprivation increases your hunger levels and increases your risk for obesity by 50 percent.

Take melatonin an hour before bedtime each night (after talking with your doctor, of course). Use deep breathing techniques to calm yourself, release toxins, evaporate anxiety, and sleep deeply. For starters, breathe in for eight seconds, hold for four seconds, then exhale for seven seconds. Read a book instead of scrolling on your phone an hour before bed. Blue light from screens triggers your body's "awake" hormones making it harder to sleep.

Here's the truth, Fear Kicker, misaligned sleep creates a misaligned life. Align your sleep to align your health.

SCAN ME

· LEARN MORE ABOUT SLEEP DEPRIVATION FROM JOHNS HOPKINS SCHOOL OF MEDICINE HERE

SPARK HABIT #6:
PRAYER AND MEDITATION

Meditation can sound boring or even freaky! But we don't have to climb a mountain or sit in a cave to benefit from it. Meditation comes from the Latin word *meditari*: to think, reflect, and consider in a present state. It is a mind-body practice that invites calm and focus, while enhancing productivity.

When I meditate, I'm inviting the Holy Spirit to fill my thoughts. I usually choose a Bible verse to slowly recite and really consider what it means, asking God to take me deeper. King David did this same thing, like he described in Psalm 119:15: "I meditate on your precepts and consider your ways."

As a related practice, I also pray for others, expressing gratitude and compassion for them. This boosts mental health and invites similar states of calm and focus to meditation. And even better, prayer changes the world! We can pray Heaven into Earth—and I think Earth could use a little more Heaven, don't you?

Turn your phone off. Close your eyes. And find focus in our age of distraction.

SPARK HABIT #7: GET GROUNDED

We'll go deeper into this Spark Habit next chapter, but earthing (or grounding) is a simple way to connect yourself with nature, God, and serious physical benefits. You walk outside every day, so why not ditch your shoes and go barefoot every once in a while?

This may be the best life hack you've never heard of. When our bodies reconnect with the earth, we improve sleep, well-being, reduce pain, and even more. Direct contact with the earth, which is more negatively charged, balances our physiology by bringing us back to a neutral charge.

Get yourself grounded every day!

Imagine a single domino on the floor. Next to it sits another domino exactly twice its size, and next to that, another that's twice the size of the second. Did you know that with just twenty-nine dominoes, each twice the size as the previous one, a single domino can knock over the Empire State Building?

This is the power of compound effects—and your spark habits are each a domino ready to set a chain reaction into motion. Pause for a moment and take a pulse check. Where are you doing well? Where do you have some structure to set? Put your plan together and get sparking!

EMBRACING SPIRITUAL STRUCTURE

Our physical health is important, but we are more than bodies. We are God's highest form of creation with eternal souls. I believe this with all my heart. And that's why embracing spiritual structure is nonnegotiable in the Wood Family.

If you don't create space and margin to nourish your spirit, you won't grow. If prayer, Bible reading, and spending time with other believers isn't a rock in your schedule, growth won't happen. And if this area of your life is weak, it will drag down every other area of your life. You will constantly feel like you're swimming against the current.

Our spiritual life is our core identity; it's truly who we are. If we miss this, we miss everything.

As a free spirit, I always wanted to be loosey-goosey and organic in my spiritual life. But here was the problem. "Organic" turned out to mean "patchy and inconsistent." My spiritual health was at the mercy of my whims. What I felt like doing determined my actions—and as a tired momma, business owner, and dreamer, that didn't serve me.

As I've matured, I've embraced the invitation to rhythm and structure. Because if I'm spiritually undernourished, it doesn't matter how well I'm doing everything else, I feel depleted. I'm like a phone that's living on 1 percent battery—not enough spark to sustain a life in service to humanity. Instead, I've discovered that living a Spirit-filled life is all about intentional time, rhythm, and structure.

Look at Jesus, for example. I don't think we could say there's ever been anyone more Spirit-filled than Him! But check this out. In Luke 5:16 we see that "Jesus often withdrew to lonely places and prayed."

He had a rhythm of getting alone with the Father. Jesus even said that He only did what He saw the Father doing (John 5:19). Jesus had a spiritual structure of pouring out and then getting poured into. And the same Father who delighted in Jesus delights in us as His children (Psalm 147:11)!

He wants to spend time with us. And that's what I've built my spiritual structure on: time with God and time with His people! There are three nonnegotiable rocks I've put in my schedule each week: Bible study, prayer, and community.

It doesn't always look the same though. Some mornings I'm reading my Bible in a comfy chair with a big cup of coffee and a notebook, scribbling down notes as the Holy Spirit blows my mind. Other days I'm scrolling through a proverb on my phone in the car after dropping off my son at school, listening to a podcast, or blaring a powerful worship song! What matters most is having a plan that fits your season of life.

PULSE CHECK

Structure doesn't mean perfection; it simply means a place. We make time for what matters most, and our spiritual lives must be at the top of the list. You've gotta give time for the Holy Spirit to fill you up. How is your spiritual structure?

EMBRACING FAMILY STRUCTURE

Doug and I always say, "You can judge our parenting when our kids are adults!" We're still in the thick of raising up amazing human beings. Even though we don't know everything, we do know what has helped our family thrive. To us, structure is based on nonnegotiables. These are the things we are going to do or not do every day, week, month, or year. One of the most important we've set up is family night.

Friday night equals family night. No calls . . . No Zooms . . . No meetings . . . It's an immovable rock in our schedule 99 percent of the time. The only exceptions are travel or periodic events. And even when those bump us out of structure, we have a plan to make up the time, and then hop right back in.

We decided this by looking at the family as a whole. There's a popular book you've probably heard of called *The Five Love Languages*. The author, Dr. Gary Chapman, describes five ways everyone gives and receives love: words of affirmation, gifts, acts of service, quality time, and physical touch.

For the Wood Family, quality time comes in at number one across the board! So that's what we've prioritized. If you came over this week, you'd definitely find me snuggling with Phoenix or Doug hugging our girls and telling them he loves them. But all of us share quality time as a main way we feel loved.

So how about your family?

The best family structures are based on giving and receiving love, communicating, "You're important to me . . . So important, I want to say 'I love you!' in a way your heart will feel." I've found the best way I can consistently do this with my children is by getting on their level!

My number one parenting tip is this: never look down on your children. Always get on their level, parenting and loving them eye-to-eye. This practice has helped me slow down and be intentional in how I raise up the next generation.

I have come to understand that our kids will remember the way

we made them feel, even through all the hard conversations. Our toughest battle as humans is not feeling seen or heard. But this one simple action models relational leadership for our kids. As they grow, they will want to tell you the tough things… the exciting things… and the fear-kicking things they have done!

There is undeniable power in locking eyes with your children, whether it is to tell them you love them or even having a firm conversation to correct certain behaviors. Getting on their level helps you call them up instead of punishing down. One of our family mantras is that we are always getting better together. These moments allow you to say, "That isn't how we do things in our family. We think and act differently."

This apple-of-our-eye connection is especially important now that our daughters are in their teen years. We regularly remind them that they are beautifully and wonderfully made, they are set apart children of God marked with a divine destiny, and the very Creator of the universe loves them eternally. And, as their mom, I will keep reminding them of these truths all the days of my life.

Last but not least, I consistently declare the words of 1 Timothy 4:12 over my kids: "Don't let anyone look down on you because you are young, but set an example for the believers in speech, in conduct, in love, in faith, and in purity." These are just some of the ways I show them how grateful and proud I am to be their Mama!

If you have kids, what does this look like for your family and your individual kiddos? If you're married, how can you arrange a structure of love for your spouse? If you have siblings, are there some fun, even nostalgic, ways you can show your care?

Make these rocks in your schedule!

Take some time right now to open your calendar or notebook and add weekly time in. Even if it starts with a one-minute block to send a text message or write a sticky note to pop on the bathroom mirror— the important thing is to *start*!

Here's the structure that's served me well. I always ask these questions to each of my people.

- On a daily basis: what do you need from me today?
- On a weekly basis: how can I be there for you this week?
- On a monthly basis: what special thing would you like to do this month?
- On a yearly basis: where would you like to go together?

Our vision as parents drives this for us. We are called to create healthy adults!

Mom or Dad, what's your vision? What's your family creed? What will the [insert your last name here] Family stand for?

Whether you're married, have kids, or are single, these are massively important questions to ask. Your answers will vibrate deep within your soul. They will be powerful enough to raise your eyes from a phone screen and see your people face-to-face. They'll help you leap out of bed and invest in creating the best version of yourself.

Why? Because your life is about more than you—and that's the most heart-filling realization people can have.

As a mom, I've watched carefully what nourishes my family best. And time after time, it comes down to the atmosphere I create. Whenever I have taken responsibility for the vibe and flow in our home, I have seen remarkable shifts in all our attitudes, conversations, and actions.

Every morning I turn on worship music that plays throughout the house. We start our days by worshiping Jesus because like it says in Psalm 118:24, "The Lord has done it this very day; let us rejoice today and be glad." Worship invites joy! I also light candles or turn on our oil diffuser so soothing smells fill the air. Every night we have prayer time with the kids. It is a rock in our schedule, helping the kids feel supported and filled with peace. This rhythm prepares them emotionally and spiritually to take on the next day.

Here is my prayer

God surround Amaya, Katelyn. and Phoenix with Your presence. May they feel Your peace that suprasses all understanding as it comes to guard their hearts & minds. Give them visions and dreams of the future you have for them. Set them apart in purity in their bodies and minds. Set Amaya and Katelyn's future husbands apart in purity and set Phoenix's wife apart in purity in body and mind. Give their parents wisdom and guidence in raising them to know You God and love You. Surround their marriages and homes tonight! In Jesus's name AMEN!

Last but not least, we also have a rhythm of chores and taking care of what we've been blessed with. Let's be honest; it's hard to embrace the idea of a worship-filled house with candles glowing in every room when you're worried there's so much crap everywhere it might catch fire! Trust me; I've had little kids. I've absolutely been there.

But for real, let me out myself right now: I am a horrible housekeeper. So when Doug started cleaning back then, that was my clue that things were getting bad! Honestly, I'm so fortunate for a dear friend who loved to clean, tidy, and organize. One day, while I was out, she swooped in like Mary Poppins and cleaned my entire house. I called her my Tinker Fairy, because she was like magic.

As our businesses have grown though, and our time has become more and more precious, I realized that I needed to stop being afraid to ask for help. I realized there are amazing people like my friend who love serving others like that and are seriously gifted at it. They're ready to step into their greatness to help you own yours. So we've hired a support team. For so many years this wasn't even a concept for me. However, our team who helps clean, organize, care for our property, and more has totally blessed our lives. The weekly structure of help is a game changer. We also help our kids see that we take care of our home via teamwork, as they each play their own part in loading the dishwasher, washing dishes, doing the laundry, picking up toys, and so on!

I understand that's not the right move for everyone. But I also know it's time for some of you reading this to hire some help.

PULSE CHECK

Here's the truth: structure is how we obtain what we want . . . In relationships . . . time . . . finances . . . and everything in between.

Isn't it amazing that we have the ability to influence generations? I'm talking about fifty-, seventy-five-, or a hundred-plus years from now. The family structure you embrace now—and keep embracing—will impact your family tree. Structure is that powerful.

Take a pulse check of yours now. Whether you feel like your family rocks here or has a long way to go, it's okay. What you start today creates a better tomorrow.

EMBRACING COMMUNITY STRUCTURE

Do you have people in your life who feel closer than family, even though they aren't related to you? I'm talking about the people in your beehive community!

Breakthrough happens in community. And even in a pandemic world, it doesn't matter if it's a virtual community, a small group, or in person. We need each other! We're not supposed to do life alone. After all, do you know what the first thing God said wasn't good? For us to be alone (Genesis 2:18).

We were created to do life together. And community has been a powerful and intentional part of Doug's and my growth. You know the saying "You become the average of the five people you spend the most time with."

So, who are you surrounding yourself with?

This may sound like tough love, but the people you invest your time in will either help you grow or hold you back. Just like intentional structure helps your family thrive, who you allow to influence your life matters if you want to win. So, over the years we've aligned with families that parent well. With couples who are going after more. And like I mentioned, we didn't always have that, so in certain seasons, we created it.

That's what we did during the COVID-19 lockdowns. Every morning for fifty days, I virtually visited a new state and hit every single one of them. We couldn't visit in-person, so we jumped into Zooms and encouraged people across the US wherever we saw leaders rising up.

Not only do we position ourselves around those who inspire us, but we want our community to have a culture of honor, respect, and inclusiveness.

Culture of Honor

We honor people's story, culture, and heritage. We're all here to lift each other up, value one another, and grow together. We honor where everyone comes from and want to assist them in where they're going. When it comes to our tribe, we all have a place at the table.

Culture of Respect

We all come with different narratives, stories, and backgrounds. We respect each other and our differing beliefs. We understand that we may believe differently on certain things, but we all still hold the same values. Beliefs can tear us apart; shared values unite us.

We surround ourselves with those who value family, relationship with God, marriage, growth, personal responsibility, and becoming the best version of themselves.

Culture of Inclusiveness

You have a place here. Full stop. This community needs your voice. We need you to own your story. We want you to join the greater mission we're pursuing in the world! Please, friend, don't do life alone. You can start by joining the movement in our Facebook community group Kick Fear in the Face.*

Today, thousands of us have joined together to kick fear in the freaking face. There is so much power in journeying together.

You have a place with us.

SCAN ME

* JOIN FELLOW FEAR KICKERS HERE

PULSE CHECK

Even though we *know* a lot of this about community, why is it so hard to *do* community sometimes? Doug and I have always known that if we didn't set up an intentional community structure, it would be too easy to isolate. To stay us four and no more (well five, with Phoenix)!

For a year and a half, we hosted weekly community gatherings in our house that we called Health and Hope Nights. We shared our stories, the areas we were contending in, and simply enjoyed each other. To this day, we call our property Breakthrough Acres. We designed it to be a place where people's lives change because *breakthrough happens in community!*

I just want you to commit to ONE

THING. Become a community starter. Read the Community Starter Manifesto out loud. Make it official. Commit yourself to creating the place and space for people to experience breakthrough. (And psst, guess what? You'll find your breakthrough, too. Promise.)

SCAN ME

˙ **MAKE THE COMMUNITY STARTER YOUR PHONE SCREENSAVER HERE**

EMBRACING FINANCIAL STRUCTURE

A little over ten years ago, Doug and I were a total financial mess. Things had been going badly in the furniture business we owned. The debt had been piling up—only I didn't know about it. I had no idea just how bad things really were.

Ready?

We were $250,000 in debt with a dying business.

Yes. A quarter of a million dollars. Talk about a reason to have an ugly cry!

The problem was that we had no financial structure. When we hit rock bottom with a mountain of debt that seemed too high to ever climb, we had to take drastic measures. For us, Dave Ramsey's Financial Peace University (FPU) was our route to the summit. FPU's seven baby steps saved our finances and became our foundational structure. And although our financial structure is different today, here's what we committed ourselves to at that time:

1. Save $1,000 for our starter emergency fund.
2. Pay off all debt (outside of our house) using the debt snowball.

Community Starter Manifesto

I am a community-starter!

I was born on this earth with
creative force and energy!
God brought me into this world and
chose my parents for a greater purpose!

I have everything I need inside of me
to bring my dreams into reality!
Community is where breakthroughs happen.
I choose to kick isolation and fear
of what people think of me in the face.

My community is looking for me and
I will create a safe place for friends
to find Home, Love, and Acceptance!
God is for me! I am loved! I am never alone!
I belong to a Community
of Creators and Inventors!

Today, I will reach out and let someone know I care!
Today I will treat my body with love and respect!
Health and Wellness are part of us!
Laughter is my medicine and together,
we will always laugh at adversity!

I am a WORLD-CHANGER and COMMUNITY-STARTER!

3. Save three to six months of expenses for a fully funded emergency fund.
4. Invest 15 percent of our income into retirement.
5. Save for our kids' education (for us, this didn't just mean college).
6. Pay off our home early.
7. Build generational wealth and become *givers*!

We stuffed cash in labeled envelopes. It was time to flex the muscle of personal responsibility in our finances. And Oh. My. Goll, was this ever hard!

One day I went grocery shopping at Trader Joe's. I frantically ran from aisle to aisle, with toddler Amaya absolutely melting down. I loaded up our cart and went to check out. And then the cashier gave me the total.

It was more money than we had. *Way* more money. I couldn't afford it.

With an impatient line of people waiting behind me and Amaya getting antsy to leave, I called Doug and asked if I could put the groceries on the credit card. If ever there was a time to make an exception, this was it, right? I mean, it was groceries, not a movie, meal out, or unnecessary toy.

On the phone, I heard Doug's voice. "No."

"What?!" I nearly shouted.

"Thea, we can't afford that. We both agreed we'd stick to our budget. We decided we aren't going to go back to the credit card lifestyle."

I wanted to argue but realized he was right. I had to shop somewhere else and get just the necessities. With tears welling in my eyes, I realized this was our reality. I picked up Amaya and left the groceries there.

I so badly wanted to get out of structure just this one time . . . But there's a reason we call it structure: there are boundaries you do not cross. Don't buck the structure. If you say you're gonna do it, do it! Stick to the program. And even though it was humiliating and I cried almost as hard as Amaya when we got to the car, Doug and I honored our commitment.

Today I know we reap the blessing, favor, and abundance directly tied to that decision and the dozens of others like it.

Here's what I learned the hard way:

IF YOUR FINANCES ARE A MESS, YOUR LIFE IS PROBABLY A MESS TOO.

Our money problems were just a symptom of underlying structural issues we had. Our health was out of control because we ate to deal with our emotions. Our finances were out of control because we spent without a balanced budget. Our debt fluffed up just like our waistlines.

Structure was the way out.

Over the last ten years, we've needed the world-class doers and entrepreneurial influencers of the world to show us what's truly possible. Our minds needed to expand into abundance thinking rather than fear. But like a patient in critical condition, you have to stop the bleeding before you buy a gym membership!

Be encouraged—if Doug and I could get out of $250,000 of personal debt, so can you. I believe there's only one thing stopping you from living in greater financial health than you are today: your lack of commitment.

Am I promising you'll be swimming in pools of cash? Or that gold will spill out of your bank account? Heck no. But I do believe a better financial position is possible for anyone who embraces personal financial responsibility and structure—and, as my friend Megan Valentine says, "do the heart work and the hard work!" This is going to take work, but I believe you can do it.

Structure propels you forward. Every time Doug and I have embraced structure in any area, we've seen our life move forward. So why do we resist it?

Surrender to the process and understand it's a good thing. It will bring an incredible blessing to your life. Yes, you might have to say no to things like Starbucks, Trader Joe's, or eating out. But it's probably stuff you don't need anyway!

Like a good friend, if you hug structure, it will hug you back.

For me, financial structure became about not putting our family in a vulnerable situation. Every time we stepped out of it, we winced and had some heartburn. For example, we purchased a Land Rover before we could really handle it financially. That decision to step out of our financial structure set us back for an entire year.

Structure isn't set-it-and-forget-it. It requires daily commitment and consistency. Every morning is a fresh chance to hold the lines you've set on your finances. What's amazing is that not only do your finances get healthier, you grow in the process as well.

While this isn't a book on finances, I do want to share one more piece of Doug and my financial structure that has blessed us greatly: giving. Even when it has hurt, we committed ourselves to generosity. This meant tithing at our church and giving toward special missions we are passionate about. Sometimes, this actually meant giving our last penny.

This lifestyle wasn't unique to us. We're riding a wave of three generations of generosity! Today, we live in the blessing of God-honoring decisions made before we were born. This is a foundation we want to build upon. Those generations modeled the biblical principle that what you sow, you will reap, like we read in Proverbs 11:24–25: "One person gives freely, yet gains even more; another withholds unduly, but comes to poverty. A generous person will prosper; whoever refreshes others will be refreshed."

Now, I'm going to share something with you. It's pretty private. And honestly, not something I would normally tell anyone else. But it's too important not to share. Doug and I have experienced incredible financial abundance from the structures we've embraced. With this blessing, we are able to support the missions we are most passionate about. Recently we hosted a Night of Awakening at Breakthrough Acres to support a pro-life women's ministry we felt called to support.

Being able to wire transfer more money than we used to earn in a year was mind-blowing. To bring a collective of people together that are passionate about life, diversity, and being change agents for future generations is why we keep showing up.

That gift has been twenty-plus years of scary obedience in the making. But it all started with things like being faithful to buy someone a cup of coffee—and the gifts have just gotten a little bigger over time.

Financial structure isn't simply about being able to buy whatever you want. It's so much more. It's about being able to write any check you feel led to. Our greatest blessing has been the gift of blessing others.

I believe you will experience this too.

I'll admit this is one of the least fun structures to embrace. Especially if, like me, you've been a free spirit most of your life. The chasing-butterflies version of Thea had to learn to cut down to the bone and stay the course. But our lives, and the generations to come, are so much better off because of it.

PULSE CHECK

Today I call myself a free spirit embracing structure. I haven't lost my spontaneity or love for adventure! What I've learned instead is that structure allows our family to flourish more than we ever could flying by the seat of our pants.

Structure determines behavior, and behavior determines the quality of our lives.

What is the overall state of your life? And which of the five structures would contribute most to raising your quality of life?

I believe embracing structure will help you say your best yes today, tomorrow, and for the rest of your life. So, what's your next move? Kick fear in the face and boldly take it!

The significant meaning behind sage

A reminder and a blessing poured over every
page in this chapter, sage represents wisdom
and protection.

CHAPTER 4

GET OUTSIDE

Have you ever had the feeling that you've reached a decision point? Like the air feels different somehow, and things are about to change? In our lives, we've learned to interpret these moments as opportunities to let go of the status quo and embrace the amazing opportunities only change can bring.

In the spring of 2014, we had the feeling that our time in Oregon was coming to a close. Doug and I went to a beautiful wedding in the wine country of Temecula, California. That weekend, Doug opened up a map of the Southwest United States and asked, "If we could live anywhere, where would you want it to be?"

We left Temecula to go home but kept the conversation going, exploring the options and starting to dream. And I'll never forget, as soon as we began our descent into Portland, the captain chimed over the speaker, informing us of strong crosswinds and pouring rain. Yep, welcome home. We realized we had to make a change.

As our coaching business had grown, we'd traveled across the country. And at that moment, places with sunshine like Texas and Arizona seemed to call us. As a family, when we left the Oregon gloom for sunshine, we thrived.

While we loved Oregon and our people there, we came home to a heaviness every time. Even though we had a wonderful life, Doug and I knew we just couldn't do it there anymore. But that was where Doug's family, our friends, and our comfort were.

If we were really going to uproot our lives, we needed a big kick fear moment. Rather than dip our toes in the water, we jumped in the deep end of the pool. A week after returning to Portland we gave notice to our landlord that we were leaving and put everything that couldn't fit into our car in storage. We didn't know where we were going—we just knew we needed to leave.

We packed up the girls, Amaya and Katelyn, and started a road trip to find home, traveling for the summer. My youngest sister had a graduation in Texas, and while it was lovely, it wasn't quite right. So, we headed to Scottsdale, Arizona. Even in the blistering heat of an Arizona summer, the desert called us.

Scottsdale it was. However, we barely knew anyone. There were a few people Doug and I knew from Masters Commission, but that was it. Our community was so far away and I felt increasingly isolated. Our Oregon friends assumed we were connected and happy because we were community starters. For six months, no one reached out to me.

Finally, after six months, my best friend from Oregon called and asked, "How are you doing, girl?!"

My immediate response: "I'm not okay!"

She felt bad for not calling but thought I'd be as busy as ever forming new relationships.

This is the season I learned firsthand that if you don't have a beehive community, it probably means you're the one who's supposed to build it.

Doug and I knew we were on the right path in Scottsdale, but it wasn't easy. It was lonely, uncomfortable, and above everything else, final. We'd made a commitment, so we weren't about to crawl home with our thumbs in our mouths!

In hindsight, it's so cool how God used this season. Our little family of four became tighter than ever. We got to know each other on a deeper level than most families have the chance to. During this time, I felt our family wasn't complete, and it took Doug some convincing over the next year to bring our son Phoenix into the world! It was two years of wandering the desert. We had each other, but that was it.

I've always been fascinated by God telling Abram to leave everything and go someplace he'd never seen before (Genesis 12). God promised to show him where to go, but he didn't give him a roadmap. Abram heard God make some big promises but had no idea what to expect. Our season of transition to Scottsdale felt like a miniature version of that.

While the fate of an entire nation wasn't on our shoulders, we did believe God had made some bold promises. During these years, I learned the power of getting grounded and getting out into nature. Connecting with God in creation—and connecting to the earth itself—saved my life.

HEALING POSTPARTUM DEPRESSION

Phoenix Michael Wood was born in October 2016, just over two years after we'd moved to Scottsdale. He was my Promised Land baby. Doug and I had gone back and forth about having a third child for years so when we finally had him, I was overjoyed. But the problem was that, much like an Oregon winter, there were dark clouds over the beauty of my life.

The first six weeks were hell.

At four weeks old we found out Phoenix had tongue-tie and lip tie, which is why he wasn't eating right or gaining weight. He had to have surgery. But even though I knew it wasn't my fault, I still felt like a failure as a mom. I couldn't even provide the nourishment my baby needed to live. That was my job, and I was failing. I'd wanted another child for so many years, but I couldn't even care for him the way I desperately wanted to.

AUNTIE JEN AT THE APPOINTMENT FOR TONGUE TIE & LIP TIE RELEASE

Every day I took a regimen of herbal supplements to encourage my milk supply. But no matter what, it just wasn't enough. I'll never forget my mother-in-law saying gently, "Thea, it's okay if you give him a bottle."

I fought it, stuck in a cycle of weighing him, feeding him, weighing him again, pumping, repeat—all this from first thing in the morning to the middle of the night, meaning sleep was nearly nonexistent. Obviously this wasn't working. So, I moved him to a bottle—and he was so happy.

"You're still a good mom, Thea," my mother-in-law said to me after the switch. "It isn't how you planned it, but it's okay."

This finally gave me some freedom to accept overnight help and sleep. We could have date nights again. But still, I felt crazy, spinning in a constant spiral of sadness and anxiety. It's a vicious, demonic cycle. At our six-week checkup, I shared that I was depressed.

"How severe?" the doctor asked.

"It's dark," I answered.

The doctor pushed a little further. "How dark?"

I took a deep breath and admitted,

"I'M SUICIDAL."

I hated having this conversation with the doctor. I hated that I felt this way with every fiber of my being. But it seemed like no matter what I did, things just kept getting worse. At this point, I couldn't even drive, and we had to hire someone to take me places when Doug was unable to.

The doctor prescribed me medication to balance me out. But I didn't feel right about the medications, so I immediately called a friend who I deeply trusted. I asked if she had any recommendations for someone else who could see me in the next twenty-four hours. Thankfully she did!

The next day I met with a woman who practiced energetic medicine—which was new to me. She immediately helped me see that my digestive system was completely out of whack, which caused my brain fog, fatigue, and a slew of other issues. Often called our second brain, our gut is responsible for producing many of the chemicals our thinking brains need to function.˙

SCAN ME

˙ **READ** *HOW THE GUT'S "SECOND BRAIN"* *INFLUENCES MOOD AND WELL-BEING* **HERE**

This gave me some fresh hope. I was starting to get answers other than a shrug and a prescription. The next day I went to see a naturopath who confirmed everything I'd learned with the energetic medicine practitioner: I was essentially septic.

As I talked further with the naturopath, it became clear that the medication was only going to mask my symptoms, not resolve them. I began multiple alternative treatments that week. For me, this was the first step toward wellness.

Please notice I say "for me." Every person is different, and we each have unique needs. We all need to do what seems best for us—but I knew that the naturopathic pathway was right for me.

As part of my new protocol, I traveled to an acupuncturist named Dr. Kim at Holy Hill for three months. I was still unwell though, so we hired someone to drive me to these appointments three times per week. However, it wasn't just needle therapy—it was the craziest treatment I've ever had.

For forty-five minutes, I sat on a pot filled with boiling tea leaves, tinctures, and herbs. Seriously, the steam smelled wild and mysterious, and as you might imagine, a bottom full of steam wasn't the most pleasant feeling. But what mattered was that the treatments were working! This process detoxified my gastrointestinal tract (and the rest of my body).

After I started seeing Dr. Kim, the clouds of depression started to break—just slightly. I had slivers of energy where I used to feel exhaustion. Dr. Kim also recommended that I "sweat every day" to continue detoxifying. So, I got my body moving outside in the Arizona sun, where it's easy to break a sweat! At the same time, I worked with a naturopath weekly for adrenal support, herbal homeopathic remedies, and Eye Movement Desensitization and Reprocessing (EMDR) Therapy.˙

SCAN ME

˙ EMDR THERAPY USES A COMBINATION OF RAPID EYE MOVEMENTS WHILE FOCUSING ON PAST TRAUMAS TO INCREASE EMOTIONAL HEALTH. YOU CAN LEARN MORE HERE

While the combination of treatments was helping, I believe these promptings to embrace alternative treatments were from God. As the Great Physician, he wanted me to schedule regular appointments in His office.

RUN FOR YOUR LIFE

Growing up, my mom was seriously diabetic, and I would often find her passed out from low blood sugar. At just five years old, I can remember having to run to get my dad, giving her orange juice, or even insulin shots. She was a strong, independent woman who hated needing anything. Not only was it terrible passing out like that, she also felt bad that she needed my help.

I remember that whenever anything felt beyond my control, like having to give my mom insulin, I'd run to my favorite place in the world, a little tree stump on our family farm. Nature was my escape. And I always found God outside.

Decades later, when I was going through my postpartum season, I knew I needed to get outside. I had to go back to my little tree stump and listen for the still small voice. Sulking inside and burying myself in movies wasn't going to lift me out of my funk. But getting outside would.

When we first moved to the Phoenix valley, we started hiking. We came to Scottsdale like fish out of water. The red rocks, cacti, and dry heat were new to us. After Phoenix was born, I took a break. But I got back into nature as soon as my postpartum treatments gave me the edge I needed to get moving.

I also ordered a jogging stroller. At first, I couldn't even run a mile. Then I found an amazing coffee shop just a little ways down the road from our house. I learned something new about myself. Not only was nature my place of healing, but I'm motivated by good coffee! I started rewarding myself with coffee at the end of each run.

Soon, I passed two miles . . . then three . . . then ten . . . then seventeen!

If you can imagine a movie montage where the superhero is training, getting better day after day, that was me. Only it was all strollers and coffee! My running journey began here. And I learned it was an endorphin rush for me. Endorphins are chemicals that make your body feel amazing and reduce the feelings of pain and even depression.

THE DIRT THAT SAVED MY LIFE

Getting outside on a run or hike always reminds me of just how big God really is. It also reminds me how incredible it is that a God that big, powerful, and awesome knows me (and you, too)! Did you know that the stars and galaxies swirling around a hundred million lightyears away don't hold a candle to us? We are God's highest form of creation. Or as Og Mandino puts it in *The Greatest Salesman in the World*, we are "nature's greatest miracle"! And when we physically connect with nature, wonderful things happen.

SCAN ME

· IF YOU WANT TO SEE HOW BIG CREATION REALLY IS, WATCH THIS VIDEO BY FRANCIS CHAN. IT WILL BLOW YOUR MIND!

SCAN ME

·· WATCH NATURE'S GREATEST MIRACLE

During my recovery from postpartum depression, nature called me out of the house and even out of my shoes. When I walked barefoot outside, I felt better. My energy was different. And again, I thought I was crazy. Why would walking outside with bare feet make a difference? I thought maybe it was because of how much time I spent running around shoeless on our farm growing up. However, the more I've studied about how to thrive in my health, the more answers I've found.

Whether we know it or not, every time our skin makes contact with the earth, we experience something called "earthing," or "grounding." Researchers in the *Journal of Environmental Public Health* define it in a study as "direct physical contact with the vast supply of electrons on the surface of the earth." And the authors of that study described why earthing seems to have positive effects on us.

SCAN ME

· GO DEEP ON THE SCIENCE OF EARTHING IN THIS JOURNAL ARTICLE

Reconnection with the earth's electrons has been found to promote intriguing physiological changes and subjective reports of well-being. Earthing (or grounding) refers to the discovery of benefits—including better sleep and reduced pain—from walking barefoot outside or sitting, working, or sleeping indoors connected to conductive systems that transfer the earth's electrons from the ground into the body.

Better sleep and reduced pain are just two of the benefits of "earthing" that researchers are uncovering. So when you're in a funk, ditch your shoes and get outdoors! Our connection to the earth, as odd as it sounds, is essential for our well-being. God made us from the dirt, after all (Genesis 2:7)!

Even as my mind and body healed, and grounding played its part, I began to understand something deeper about myself (and you too). We are miracles, uniquely made and specially chosen. Before we were born, God knew us. He has a purpose for us—and it is to thrive!

THE APPLE OF GOD'S EYE

Even out of all the Arizona beauty I surrounded myself with, I realized that we, as His children, are His true delight. Have you ever heard someone say, "You're the apple of my eye"? It actually comes from David in Psalm 17:8: "Keep me as the apple of your eye; hide me in the shadow of your wings."

As a kid I wondered, "Why in the world does God have an apple in

His eye?!" But when you study Hebrew, that phrase is awe-inspiring. Imagine yourself as a child, nose to nose with your mom or dad, wrapped in a big hug. If you were to look straight into your parent's eyes, you'd see your own reflection. Your face would become the apple of their eye.

For me, as a child, there was no place safer than my mom's or dad's arms. And that's what David asks God: to keep him so close and cherished that they'd be nose to nose.

My friend, the God who flung the stars from His fingertips created you as a light to shine just as bright. I believe He's placed a contender spirit in each of us to pursue more every single day. So whatever trial you're going through—depression, addiction, cancer, divorce, disappointment, or any deep sorrow—know this: God has a unique plan in your life.

The earth is God's footstool, but He's got bigger plans for us than to prop up His feet! He wants to do mighty things through you and me. The more I've found awe in God's power and miracles revealed in nature, the more I trust Him with every part of my life.

On the farm, there was a special place up on a hill my dad showed us girls when we were young. There was something about how the land contoured around it, forming a natural amphitheater. It was special because when you shouted there, your voice could be heard anywhere on our land! It was like magic. We knew if we were ever afraid or in trouble, we could run to the hill and call for our dad, and he would hear and be right there.

For me, spending time outside was like a call for God's help. It was part of my mental, physical, and spiritual healing. And just like my voice echoed across the farm as a little girl, God's response echoes through my life: "You are chosen, loved, and divinely placed on this Earth for such a time as this!"

I believe God wants to show us His power, but also His closeness. He wants to give us a broader perspective, but also realize every hair on our head is numbered. And nature is one heck of a meeting place. Get outside, listen for God's voice, and experience some healing that's just waiting for you to take the first step. (Without shoes, of course!)

Luke 4: 18-19

"The Spirit of the Lord is on me, because he has anointed me to proclaim good news to the poor. He has sent me to proclaim freedom for the prisoners and recovery of sight for the blind, to set the oppressed free, to proclaim the year of the Lord's favor."

CHAPTER 5

SPIRIT BREAK OUT

Have you ever been in a season where life didn't seem like heaven on earth?

You're doing all the right things: going to church, reading your Bible, loving on your people, pressing into your tribe, praying hard, and flexing your hustle muscle. But still, breakthrough just won't come. In fact, it might seem farther away than ever before.

A number of years ago, this was me. My mother-in-law (who I call my mom-in-love) battled cancer. My family fought old addictions. My parents contended to keep the family farm. Life threw us curveball after curveball, and we kept striking out.

I was frustrated, even angry. "This isn't how it's supposed to be," I thought. We're supposed to walk in blessing and abundance. But here we were, stuck in cycles of crappiness.

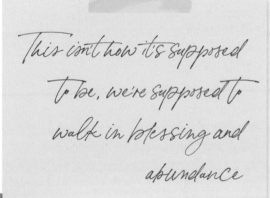

This isn't how it's supposed to be, we're supposed to walk in blessing and abundance

What does it mean when the "right" things don't seem to work? When God seems far away? Or friends don't act much like friends at all, even though you've been showing up for them? Or even when the scale won't budge despite you eating perfectly?!

Does this sound at all like seasons you've lived through? It might even be a season you're in right now. I've had to learn over and over again that kicking fear in the face isn't a one-and-done practice. It's a muscle we choose to flex every day. Because life isn't tame, is it? It's wild. Wonderful and beautiful at times, with majestic mountain top views. Other times it's dark, like the valley of the shadow of death David wrote about in Psalm 23.

It's in the valleys that we are made. We act our way out of fear. After all, we can only learn courage when we face something we're afraid of. In times like these that I've been through—and am going through even as I write this—I've learned a powerful practice.

Proclamation. It is a powerful act with deep meaning. Merriam-Webster defines it in a few different ways:

> "To declare publicly, typically insistently, proudly, or
> defiantly and in either speech or writing;
> to give outward indication of;
> to praise or glorify openly or publicly."

Proclamation is a tool for every Fear Kicker in any time, place, or season. And it completely changed my life because it brought me into radical encounters with God.

THE PRACTICE OF PROCLAMATION

As the Jesus Freak girl, I grew up with Scripture. Lots of it! I memorized verses, sang them in worship songs every day, and even prayed through them. But in this tough season of my family battling illness, addiction, and financial hardship, simply reading the Bible, singing the songs, and praying the prayers felt flat. They lacked a vibrancy and power that I had experienced so many times before.

I cried out to God, "Why can't I just tap back into Your power?!"

Then I saw something I'd never seen before. Even though I'd read this passage a thousand times before, even memorizing it, it was like it came to life. Jesus stepped out of the pages and into my circumstances.

Have you ever heard of the Lord's Prayer?

Even if you didn't grow up in church and revivals like me, chances are you've heard it in songs, movies, and even books. It's probably the most famous prayer of all time. Here's how it happened.

Jesus picked twelve disciples. They were ordinary guys. Not the cream of the crop kinda people either. They weren't rich. They weren't well-connected. And they definitely weren't social media influencers!

One day, Jesus was praying in a special spot he prayed at all the time. One of his disciples watched him pray and thought something like, "Man, I've never seen anyone pray like that. I wonder if he could teach us?"

So, he went up to Jesus and asked Him, "Lord, teach us to pray . . ."

Jesus turned to these men and women—this gang of misfits and disruptors, hungry for more—and shared this way of praying with them.

What was amazing is that Jesus expected them to pray *and* believed they could experience powerful prayer!

Jesus started like this: "When you pray . . ."

When I read this slowly, I saw that Jesus expected His disciples to pray. That meant He expected me to pray. And He wouldn't expect me to pray if there wasn't something powerful within my grasp. (And I believe within yours too.)

Here's how He started in Luke 11:2: "Our Father, in heaven Hallowed be Your name" (NKJV).

Jesus proclaimed that there is a Father in heaven who knows our name! Even though He was in heaven and seemed a thousand miles away in that dark season, He was just a conversation away. He was near to me like a father and his daughter. I have a relationship with and access to Him.

This realization, that God knows me and loves me like a good dad, rocked my world. And during this time, an amazing song came out by Kim Walker-Smith called "Spirit Break Out." And wouldn't you know it . . . it starts with the Lord's Prayer. This was a Scripture I had grown up with, but through this amazing song, it came alive! In the middle of everything going on I could proclaim, "You're good. You're faithful. You're giving me everything I need today!"

I learned to proclaim and rediscover that contender spirit. You see, I encountered the Holy Spirit when I was seven years old, even receiving a new prayer language, like Paul talked about in 1 Corinthians 14:2: "For anyone who speaks in a tongue does not speak to people but to God. Indeed, no one understands them; they utter mysteries by the Spirit."

I sang along with Kim Walker-Smith. I proclaimed God's promises,

power, and presence. And you know what, the cancer didn't leave in one day—it took two years. Our family addictions didn't just evaporate —we're still contending. But I learned to proclaim in the midst of the storm.

I met Jesus as the Great Storm Breaker, like the disciples did on the Sea of Galilee (Mark 4:35–41). I knew He was going to make a way, even in the wilderness. That's the promise I held on to over everything else.

SPIRIT-LED, NO MATTER WHAT!

I learned to operate in that kind of Spirit-led life. And let me tell you, sometimes it had its quirks.

Sometimes the things God asks us to do seem random. They leave you wondering, "Okay God, but why?" Other times, they seem small, like bringing coffee to people, sending flowers, or even just a random text to encourage someone. Like if you didn't do it, who would care? No one would even know the difference.

I remember once waking up in the middle of the night when my mom was in the hospital. There was an urgency in my gut to go to the hospital and pray for her—at 3 a.m.!

But I had learned to obey IMMEDIATELY. So I jumped up, threw some clothes on, and drove to the hospital. I tiptoed quietly into my mom's room so I wouldn't wake her up and prayed. Not a simple "God, please heal her if you're feeling nice today." But a proclamation.

> God of angel armies, You are breaking down walls of resistance. You are defeating the powers and principalities that are coming against us. You are healing this woman's body. You are bringing victory into this house. Our family is rising up on eagle's wings. You are doing a new thing in us and through us. You are breaking through in every area of our lives!

Now, you might be thinking, "That's great for you, Thea. But how

Our Father, all of heaven roars Your Name

Sing louder, let this place erupt with praise

Can you hear it, the sound of heaven touching earth

The sound of heaven touching earth

Spirit break out

Break our walls down

Spirit break out

Heaven come down

King Jesus, You're the name we're lifting high

Your glory, shaking up the earth and skies

Revival, we want to see Your kingdom here

We want to see Your kingdom here

SCAN ME

' LISTEN TO SPIRIT BREAK OUT PERFORMED
BY KIM WALKER-SMITH

on earth am I supposed to know where to go in the middle of the night . . . or how to pray . . . or who to buy a coffee for?"

Here's my promise to you: you will know! And I can promise you because Jesus promised that to both of us in Luke 12:12: "for the Holy Spirit will teach you at that time what you should say."

One of my dearest friends and pastors, Ashli Van Horn, is wonderful at this. Recently, it was another doozy of a season in certain places. (Because remember, hard times don't go away!) But she felt like God gave her a Scripture for me. It was Isaiah 30:21: "Your ears will hear a word behind you, 'This is the way, walk in it,' whenever you turn to the right or to the left." (NLV)

It could not have been more perfect timing.

I was speaking at an event for a summer tour my family went on called the Massive Momentum Tour (I'll share the whole crazy story in chapter 17). And as I spoke, I literally felt a tapping on the shoulder. In that moment, God led me totally off-topic and I shared something special just for those people at that time.

When I got home, that tapping and guiding continued. I kept hearing that Scripture echo, "This is the way, walk it . . ." I was compelled to throw away books and cards and materials that I knew would try and lead me off the path the Holy Spirit had for me. This was wild, and Doug probably thought I was crazy because my trash cans filled with resources I knew weren't true.

I promise you, God is clear. You will know what to do, what to say, and where to go! He is a God that taps us on the shoulder and points the way. He clears our path. And sometimes that means clearing out some garbage that wants to pull you down.

I promise you, God is clear. You will know what to do.

THE SECRET PLACE

Here's the truth, Fear Kickers: the same spirit that raised Christ from the dead lives in you.

There was a knowing deep inside of me. And Kim Walker-Smith's song was exactly what I needed. It was the song, sound, frequency, and energy that pulled me scary close to God's glory. To this day, that song draws me in a special way to the inner courts of heaven itself.

David wrote about this place and his longing to live there. He told God in Psalm 27:4, "One thing I ask from the LORD, this only do I seek: that I may dwell in the house of the LORD all the days of my life, to gaze on the beauty of the LORD and to seek him in his temple."

I FIND MY SECRET PLACE WHEN I AM IN NATURE

David wanted to be in the secret place with God, in complete surrender, gazing at His beauty. And just a few chapters later, we find more amazing inspiration from David. He wrote in Psalm 34:8, "Taste and see that the LORD is good; blessed is the one who takes refuge in him."

This is a proclamation we make and a refuge we can take!

David wrote these words about God's goodness and the blessing in His protective presence in a cave called Adullam. We'd usually think of a cave as a deep, safe, secret hideout. But this cave wasn't really safe at all.

The full story is in 1 Samuel 22. David was hiding from King Saul, who was obsessed with killing him. Even though David had done nothing but good to King Saul and was even best friends with his son, the king was threatened by him. It was so dangerous, David even had to send his family away in secret. But still, desperate in that cave, David proclaimed God's goodness, and knew He was the true safe place.

We know the rest of the story—but in the moment, David had no clue how things would end. But God saved David, eventually putting him on the throne. And generations later, a new king was born out of David's tribe of Judah: Jesus!

Let's get busy serving our God and people like David. Because in that cave, the people who came to his rescue weren't even the benchwarmers. At best, they were the water boys: "All those who were in distress or in debt or discontented gathered around him, and he became their commander. About four hundred men were with him" (1 Samuel 22:2).

The distressed . . . the debtors . . . the discontented. Not a very helpful group of people, right? However, David became their leader. He loved them and served them.

Proclamation doesn't guarantee unicorns and rainbows. In fact, sometimes God tells us to show up for people that make us think, "But God, I don't need another project in my life!" However, when I've obeyed immediately and shown up to serve (even when I didn't feel like it), the Holy Spirit whispered, "I am mentoring you."

BREAKTHROUGH WILL COME

I learned to ask, "God, what are we going to do today?"

Even though I might not have seen an end in sight, this question always gave me a glimmer of light ahead. It was a little lamp that gave me just enough light to keep walking. I felt the Spirit of God deep in my bones, and my faith kept building, day after day.

"God, what are we going to do today?"

That's right . . . "We," not "me.

"God, what are we going to do today?"

The Holy Spirit spoke, and there was no one who could tell me He wasn't real.

I proclaimed. I sang. I worshiped with Kim Walker-Smith over and over again. (Seriously, go listen to this song right now!)

Everything you want, everything you're made for, every victory for every battle is on the other side of fear. Form the habit of kicking it in the face with God! Lean on His promises. Embrace His perfect love that casts out fear (1 John 4:18)!

Like for David, things don't magically get easier. In fact, I remember days of driving people to get WIC while doing coaching calls with my clients. At the same time, Doug's parents were divorcing.

Even when you live a surrendered life, the natural realm can look very messy. But heaven will break into your life as you partner with God. Keep leaning in. Keep contending. Your breakthrough is coming—and it will come through proclaiming and living in God's power.

Even when God's invitation is in the small things, the mundane things, the insignificant things, you're taking exactly the steps you need to take.

A cocoon doesn't look very flashy, does it? A caterpillar wraps itself in an ugly husk. It's drab, dull, and certainly not something we'd ever hang up in our living rooms. Who wants a crumbly shell holding a fat little worm?! But we know what lies beyond the cocoon, don't we?

The butterfly is only born out of struggle.

If you take the developing butterfly out of its cocoon too soon— removing the hardship, the flexing—it will die. That's because it gets the strength it needs to fly from the struggle of emerging. God has provided a path for every caterpillar to become a butterfly. But it definitely isn't sexy!

That's my story. No one else could create my breakthrough. The struggle was mine to contend with. The fear was a cocoon; ugly and bland. It had wrapped itself around me. But as I proclaimed God's power, His strength kept developing within me. Every day for six months, I met the Lord. I proclaimed His goodness and breakthrough, even when the natural looked anything but good.

So many times, we see someone further along the trail than we are and imagine that poof, they suddenly appeared there. They're already up the mountain because they're special. Not like us, starting at the trailhead miles away from the summit. We think breakthroughs happen all of a sudden—but no way is that true.

There's no elevator in this skyscraper! It happens by climbing one step at a time.

Those steps are small and there are a lot of them. Progress seems slow, but to keep my mind out of negative cycles, my perspective had to shift.

I proclaimed that healing was going to come.

AND I BELIEVED.

I proclaimed there would be restoration in our marriage.

AND I BELIEVED.

I proclaimed God's provision would calm the storms.

AND I BELIEVED.

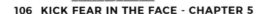

Dear LORD Jesus,

I come before your throne of grace, love, and mercy. Knowing that every dream and desire is in the hands of my KING and Master. LORD, I want to be whole heartly in love with you. I give you my whole life that you can use me for the plans & purposes you have for me. I desire to step up to the position I know you want me to be, and worship and dance whole-heartly before your throne. I never want to stop praising, loving, and giving you glory every minute of everyday. I want to be a WOMEN of GOD, knowing in my heart that I have and am going to study your word daily. I want to learn diligence more this year than ever before. LORD, I pray that my heart of worship would come forth this year than ever before. That as I dance before you, LORD Wholeheartly, people would come to know you through that. I commit my life this day to your greater purposes. That I would became the bride & continue to life for you daily even after this year. LORD, I am here to learn your plans for my future & to hide you OH, LORD in my heart. So, that it can never be taken away. Prepare me for my future husband, that I will be a virtuous woman... I know your desires for me are bigger than I can ever imangie GOD show Yourself to me more than I've ever known & so that the light of You would shine through me. Take all of me; my pride of being so pure, LORD use that purity for something... I know you have kept me for I main purpose. For my husband, on my wedding night, let that minister to someone (you know)!! LORD with my whole heart I want to be a true worshiper worshiping you in spirit & truth, for I know you seek such worshipers. HUMBLE ME THIS YEAR MORE than ever. That after this year I would have more of a heart for High School students all over America. (One thing LORD this year more than anything is to love you and see souls touched). This is one dream seeing 500 people with banners praising your NAME. I want to have a double portion of the WORSHIPER HEART.

LOVE YOUR DAUGHTER. Thus Marea. Thank you LORD. Jesus.

WHAT WILL YOU PROCLAIM?

At the beginning of Masters Commission, when I was just nineteen years old, I wrote something we called a Covenant Letter to God. Doug wrote one too. It was a declaration of commitment, intention, and surrender. We were each totally giving ourselves to God for the next year—and ultimately, for life.

I still have this letter, and as I read it today, I see how God has made it come true.

I wrote a Covenant Letter to this God of provision! If you were to write a letter to God, committing your life in a covenant relationship (which means no matter what comes your way, you're all-in), what would it say?

Take some time to worship, think, meditate, pray, and proclaim. Let the Holy Spirit open your mind to the cocoon He wants to develop you in this next year. Grab your journal and let the words in your heart flow onto the page.

I believe you're reading this book because God has massive plans for you, your family, and your community. I believe you are a Fear Kicker, a world-changer, and a chain-breaker. I believe that no weapon formed against you will stand. And I proclaim victory is already yours if you walk in step with the Spirit, asking this simple question: "God, what are we going to do today?"

Now, let me share with you more of what He might have in store.

Big Mac Salad

Ingredients:
2 1/2 cups lettuce, shredded 1/4
cup tomatoes, chopped
4.5 ounces lean 95 - 97% ground
beef, cooked
1/4 cup reduced fat shredded
cheddar cheese
2 dill pickle spears, chopped
1 tbsp onion, chopped
1/2 tsp sesame seeds

Dressing:
2 tbsp Wish-bone Lite Thousand
Island Dressing
1/8 tsp white wine vinegar
1/8 tsp onion powder
Optional ~ a little sprinkle of stevia

Directions:
Combine dressing ingredients in a bowl, then set aside. Mix lettuce, tomatoes, ground beef, cheese, pickles, and onion in a separate bowl. Top with your favorite dressing, sprinkle on sesame seeds, and enjoy with family or friends!

CHAPTER 6

BRING THEM A LEAN & GREEN

Doug and I had just won an all-inclusive trip to Cabo San Lucas, Mexico as a reward for our coaching business's growth.

From the beautiful oceanfront resort to the sapphire blue water rimmed with white beaches, the experience was extravagant. I remember drinking in the feeling of rest as my every need was taken care of.

At this point in our marriage, we had rarely traveled without our children, so this felt like a second honeymoon for us! The kids took up most of my brain space on a daily basis, and while I would make that sacrifice every single time, this short break from mom life was just what I needed to recharge my batteries and refocus my vision.

We had worked hard and helped a multitude of business partners earn this same trip. While that was satisfying, I was feeling the strain of being a mompreneur. We had shut down our retail furniture storefront at this point, but we still had a second furniture warehouse business. Add our two young children on top of it all, and it was a recipe for exhaustion.

The struggle was real. Doug and I lived right on the edge as we burned the candle at both ends. I don't remember a lot of the trip because I was so sleep-deprived. Needless to say, naps under big umbrellas on Cabo beaches were calling my name.

Part of the all-inclusive vacation were these group mini adventures. Now, I'm not a big excursion person. You won't catch me hiking through the jungle with a machete or anything. However, this one was a short bus ride to the docks for a yacht ride. I could get on board with that!

We piled into a tiny bus with a crowd of other people, and I ended up sitting on Doug's lap because we were squashed like sardines. But the moment the bus started rumbling down the dirt road, our fellow travelers stood up on the moving bus and crowded around us. We were further along in our business than most, so they looked up to us for advice, asking questions like:

"How do you do what you do?"

"How have you helped so many people?"

"What's the sauce to your success?"

I remember one guy who scooted up next to us like a kid on Christmas morning, asking for similar advice. But when I answered him, I could see the twinkle vanish from his eyes.

"Thea, how do I get more clients?" he asked.

I answered automatically, "Just bring them a lean and green."

He stared at me blankly.

Doug chuckled and said, "Thea, you have to explain what that means."

I shrugged and explained like it was the most obvious thing in the world.

"If there's a family in need, or I get an email about the mommy meal train, or somebody's mom is battling cancer . . . I just bring them a healthy meal. All you have to do is serve and support people. Genuinely love on them. This builds trust because they know you're authentically in their corner. It's not about 'getting' people, it's about caring and connecting. That's it. It's really that simple."

The guy seemed genuinely confused. He responded with an unconvinced, "Okay . . ."

I could tell that he was a little disappointed. But whether he liked it or not,

serving others is the key to any door.

To be honest, I still don't know how to make it any simpler. If you're in the business of "getting" people, you're only going to make things harder on yourself. People are smart. They have sensitive radars that detect when someone wants something from them. So, what if instead of trying to get all the time, we just tried to give?

ON THE HOOK

If you're in business of any kind, you've probably heard about the need to "hook" people. I don't mean getting them addicted to anything. It's a term about grabbing and keeping people's attention so you can make them customers. But I once heard it explained in a different way by author Seth Godin, which totally flipped the script.

He talked about a generous practice he saw in Turkey while visiting. Being "on the hook" took a whole new meaning. He explained that when people buy a loaf of bread at their local bakery, those with the financial means buy a second loaf, and the baker hangs that second loaf on a hook for people without enough money to eat.

I haven't seen any force for growing a business, ministry, or anything else more powerful than serving people well. What if we showed up looking for opportunities to give instead of get?

One of my favorite stories about Jesus is about exactly this. In John 13, the disciples are showing up for dinner. In those days, they didn't have nice paved roads like us, so they walked around in sandals, getting dirt, mud, and the smelly animal stuff on their feet and ankles. Yuck!

So when people in that culture entered someone's home, a servant would wash their feet with fresh water from a basin, then towel them dry. It was their version of taking their muddy boots off before walking into someone's living room. This wasn't a job for important people.

That was why it was so crazy that the disciples arrived to see Jesus kneeling down, towel around his waist, basin on the floor, ready to wash their feet. Jesus didn't act like the kind of leader who thought he was more important than everyone else. He acted like a servant, ready to help and clean even though it wasn't his job.

Jesus showed up with generosity, not an agenda.

Imagine yourself walking around with Jesus's towel and basin as you come into each new situation. You cannot believe the doors that will be opened to you when you lay aside your own agenda and come to people with the open hand and willing heart of Jesus.

SERVE YOUR WAY TO SUCCESS

Do you want to grow a business, ministry, or anything else? It all starts in the same place: a posture of serving. The energy you put out will come back to you again and again. Service builds trust as it breaks down walls of resistance. Today, everyone will put up walls, feeling like you're probably coming with an agenda—until you serve them.

If you come to people with pure intentions, they'll want to partner with you. More than that, they'll want to hang out with you because you make their life better. After all, who do you like spending time with? People who make everything about themselves, or those who are genuinely interested in you?

This mindset has been vital to our success in every area of life and business.

So, when business owners or entrepreneurs come to me for advice, they often ask me how to "get" people. That question needs to be flipped on its head. It's not about "getting" people. It's about *serving people.*

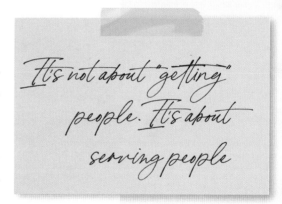

It's not about "getting" people. It's about serving people

HOW TO SHOW UP

If you want to cultivate the heart of a servant and grow your success, here's my challenge: don't let another kind thought slip by without action! When a friend, parent, or coworker pops into your head, order

those flowers. Deliver that lunch. Show up with that coffee. Send that text message. Make that call! Don't second-guess yourself. When people are going through hard times, what's the best thing you can do for them? Love them. Serve them. Bring them a lean and green.

It's kind of funny, but success starts with the smallest of seeds.

Now, I can hear the excuses already. "I don't have time for that! Nobody would want to eat my cooking! People will think it's weird!"

In this day and age, sending a kind gift has never been easier! Sending flowers is just a few clicks away. You don't have to be a chef; in fact, I'm not a cook at all. Providing lunch to someone is as simple as ordering food into their workplace. My daughter, Amaya, sends coffees and treats to her friends all the time, and she's only in high school!

Stop the excuses and start serving people.

Let me be clear: I don't want you to start spending unwisely. If you don't have the money right now, don't buy stuff outside of your budget. (Remember my moment at Trader Joe's?) At the same time, never underestimate even the smallest amount of time, money, or affection that you have to give.

There's another beautiful Jesus story I love in Mark 12:41–44. Jesus sat down in front of the offering box at the temple. He watched a bunch of rich people toss in huge sums of money. Then a poor old widow shuffled up to the box and put in two insignificant copper coins. Today, they would equal less than a penny. How could this matter?

Jesus gathered His disciples all around Him and said, "I tell you the truth, this poor widow has put more into the offering box than all the others. For they all gave out of their wealth. But she, out of her poverty, put in what she had to live on, everything she had."

Beautiful! I can sympathize with this story because I have felt the same way as that old widow. There was a season of my life where I didn't have much to give. I was dealing with a lot of struggles in my family. On top of that, my internal dialogue was a narrative of limiting beliefs. Despite all the stressors dragging me down, I decided to take action on the small things. Every time God gave me an opportunity to serve, I gave what I had. He was training me to never let a kind thought fade away without action.

Faithful servanthood has led me to being entrusted with more. I developed my habit of kindness when I had little to give, and now God has multiplied it into so much more.

You don't need to elevate yourself or your business. You need to walk like Jesus with a towel in hand to serve and succeed at the highest level. If you can go out with that energy, just watch what happens in your life.

Be faithful to look for opportunities to serve, especially when nobody's looking. Act like it's not the worker at the grocery store's job to put your cart away. Putting your cart away is your job. If you think it's not your job, well, it's even more important that you make it your job because that me-first mindset is probably why you're not getting the breakthrough you want in your life!

Serve your way to success.

I'll be honest though. Serving people is A LOT of work. It's hard. We have to fight our own selfish impulses and embrace inconvenience. I'm not this wonderful angel of a person who walks around like Mother freakin' Teresa! It takes work. But it's worth the effort every time.

WHERE DO YOU GET SO MUCH FLIPPIN' ENERGY?

People ask me all the time where I get so much energy. I always reply the same way: "I have never known a life without Jesus, and He gives me the grit to fight through."

God has given you everything you need. You have a divine connection. There is a Father who loves and sees you. He understands everything about you. And He does the same for everyone you meet.

I believe that everybody has this power source available because the very power that raised Jesus from the dead can live inside you. If you can grasp the implications of that statement fully, you will never encounter a problem bigger than the power inside you.

As a Midwest farm girl, I learned a good work ethic. We did hard things in my family like baling hay, picking rocks, and doing endless chores. This kind of living gave me deep wells of grit to draw from. So, where do I get all this flippin' energy? I put in the work and God meets me there with His work gloves on too.

GOD GOES HIP-TO-HIP WITH THE PEOPLE WILLING TO PARTNER WITH HIM.

I don't have a quitter's bone in my body, and I don't believe you have any quit within you either.

When people want to quit their dreams, it isn't always because they're tired. Sometimes it's because they're scared. It's because of that narrative constantly chattering in their heads. "What if I'm not good enough? What if I'm dumb? What if no one likes me? What if . . . ?"

Ready for your secret weapon?

Do it afraid! Action diffuses fear.

Does this even matter? Does all this talk about grit and not giving up really matter to my daily life? Does it actually impact my Spark Habits, acts of service, and relationships?

Yes! All of it matters. It's all connected to the breakthrough you're looking for. The problem starts when we're not tapping into the full access that we've been given through Jesus.

So, Jesus follower, have you really surrendered your whole life? If you feel like your power is cut off, it may be because you're disconnected from the source. I don't know about you, but my phone dies when I don't charge it. I have to plug it in to power it up. Our spirits, minds, and souls are the same way.

I want to help you go after all that God has put you on this earth to do. The trick is learning to surrender and fully rest in His flow. Whenever I start to take things wholly into my own hands, things get really hard. They get confusing. But God brings the support and divine connection into my path when I dig deep and surrender all of myself.

THROUGH THE STORMS

Let's take a timeout for a second.

I want to make sure you don't think I'm saying that if you serve people and put out good energy, no bad things are ever gonna happen. That's a fake promise to me, and it's not what I believe. Let's be real. I pointed us to Jesus. He was the greatest servant and positive energy force of all. But He was still crucified! We're in the arena, my friends.

I'm saying, despite the bad things happening right now, you can move forward in the midst of them. That's the promise of God. Despite the storm clouds and setbacks, you can keep moving forward. And just like we talked about, He will turn those pain points into purpose points. You will find the power to own your story, deliver some lean and greens, and change some lives in the process. God promises over and over that He will always protect, guide, and support His kids.

Understand that just because you bring someone a lean and green or a coffee, you can't say, "I did my good boy or girl thing. Now my life is gonna be like Mary Poppins."

You don't plant a seed today and start picking apples tomorrow. There is a growth period before the harvest. Are you ready for the growth season? For showing up and planting seeds—probably thousands of them—before you get to walk through your apple orchard?

The Bible tells us that the harvest is plentiful but the workers are few (Matthew 9:37), and I've taken this verse to heart. It's gonna take work! But every time I make my life and business about serving others, I experience amazing growth and impact on this journey. And you can too! It may not happen immediately, but it will come And as sure as a seed grows into a flower, your love and commitment will bloom into divine connection and thriving relationships.

BE GENEROUS, THEN NEVER STOP

When I look back at the over three hundred thousand people Doug and I have been able to help, I can barely believe it. I'm crazy humbled. But just like I told the guy on that bumpy bus ride in Cabo, every one of those changed lives started with a lean and green, an act of service, love, and generosity. So on the days I feel hard-pressed on every side (which never stops, by the way), I'm reminded of the incredible good showing up when you don't feel like it does in the world. This always lifts my perspective and helps me tap into that God energy.

The harvest is *plentiful,* but the *laborers are few*

Luke 10:2 & Matthew 9:39

This reminds me of a season where a dear friend and I started to grow apart. I started sending her little bracelet charms and handwritten letters via snail mail. We rarely talked. But I just kept sending her these little acts of kindness.

Almost two years later, we ended up together at a women's retreat. And I noticed she had on the cutest piece of jewelry.

"Oh my goodness, I love your necklace!" I said.

She replied, "These are all the charms you sent me. I collected them on this necklace!"

We had an incredible moment of connection that would have been impossible without the seeds of kindness planted. I was just obedient to do my part, and God rekindled a relationship that is so important to me.

Baby steps of kindness, the little things we do when we bring what we have, create highways of opportunity. The destination isn't instantaneous, but the journey is worth it.

Jesus called His disciples into literal storms twice. He wasn't surprised by the storms. In fact, He slept through most of the first one documented in the Bible. I can only imagine the disciples fearing for their lives while Jesus was cat napping in the back of the boat. He came out on deck, and repeated what He had said over a hundred times in the gospels, "Do not be afraid." Then He said to the storm, "Peace, be still." The wind calmed, the water became smooth as glass, and they were safe.

Apparently Jesus thought they needed the lesson again because he called them into another storm! Jesus sent them across a lake while He went to pray. A storm came up on the lake, so Jesus decided to walk out to them. They were terrified and believed Jesus was a ghost walking across the water. Jesus knew their fear and repeated His theme: "Do not be afraid."

Life isn't always smooth sailing, but the storms and the miracles go hand in hand. You have to lean in and surrender to the process to find your miracle in the storm.

When you feel like giving up . . . When you feel like you don't have any more energy . . . I want you to know there is someone kneeling down at their bedside pleading with God for a miracle in their storm. Your action could be the answer to that miracle. There's always life on the other side of the pain you're feeling.

So often, the fastest way out of your pain is encouraging, loving, or serving someone else. And when you do so, not only does it bless their life, but it blesses yours as well.

I'll never forget that amazing trip to Cabo San Lucas—not because of our yacht ride, but because of the bus ride. I don't know if that guy ever took my oddball advice seriously. But I promise, if you join me in showing up for others, wearing that servant's towel around your waist, ready to wash muddy feet, everything will change.

Blessing waits just around the corner. It's usually just disguised as an act of kindness for someone else!

CABO SAN LUCAS

Proverbs 26:20

"It takes fuel to have a fire— a fire dies down when you run out of fuel. So quarrels disappear when the gossip ends." (TPT)

CHAPTER 7

NO DRAMA ZONE

Some of you really like drama. I mean, you really like it—so much it's become an addiction. I know because I'm a recovering dramaholic!

See if any of this sounds like you or someone you know. Even though you say you hate it, you're always surrounded by drama. The people in your life constantly let you down. You find yourself talking about other people behind their back (a lot). Your long list of problems are always someone else's fault:

They didn't come through like they said they would.

They didn't support you when you needed it.

They get all the recognition for your hard work.

Or maybe your life looks more like this: You have to wear a superhero cape every other day. When people come to you with their problems, you take it as a personal mission to rescue them. After all, they need your help—it's the right thing to do! However, one problem snowballs into another until your circle looks like a soap opera.

Remember what we talked about in Chapter 2: Beehive Community? Your vibe attracts your tribe. And if you're the source of drama, guess what? You'll be surrounded by drama kings and queens!

The drama lifestyle is draining. It's toxic. We know this . . . right? So why are so many of us dramaholics (like I used to be)? Because drama is a drug, y'all!

Drama drives the same highways in our brains as addictive stuff like nicotine, alcohol, or crack. For real—drama addicts like opiates. And like any addiction, science shows that we build up a tolerance to it, meaning we crave more and more hits of drama to keep our high.˙

SCAN ME

˙ **LEARN MORE ABOUT THE FASCINATING SCIENCE OF DRAMA ADDICTION HERE**

Drama triggers our pituitary gland and hypothalamus to crank out endorphins. Those are the feel-good chemicals that suppress pain and increase pleasure. Again, like drugs!

So first of all, as a former dramaholic, I want to welcome you to the circle. Up to this point, if you didn't realize your drama problem, it's not your fault. However, if you're totally honest with yourself and are a source of drama like I was, it is now your responsibility to live above drama, draw a do-not-cross line, and then hold your ground like your life depends on it.

That sounds amazing, right? Let's do it together. (And PS, if you've got a dramaholic in your circle, make sure the book is out on your table and just happens to be open to this chapter! I got you.)

WHICH WOLF WILL YOU FEED?

There once was a boy walking with his grandfather, who was a respected, very successful businessman in their city. As they walked and talked about life, the boy asked, "Grandpa, how did you become so successful?"

His grandfather replied, "What do you mean by successful?"

The boy answered, "Well, you're generous, people look up to you, you always spend Saturday mornings with me, and you can do whatever you want. That seems pretty successful to me."

"The secret isn't what I achieved," his grandpa said, "the secret is in who I had to become. Everything else took care of itself."

Confused, the boy asked, "What do you mean?"

"Everyone has two wolves inside of them: the drama wolf and the dreamer wolf. The drama wolf wants constant attention and needs others to constantly praise them to love itself. The dreamer wolf, on the other hand, is obsessed with creation. It is curious and constantly working to grow, create opportunities, and empower others."

The boy listened, then asked, "So, what happens with them?"

"They fight," his grandpa answered.

"Which one wins?"

His grandpa smiled and said, "The one you feed, my boy, the one you feed."

So, Fear Kicker, which wolf are you feeding? The drama or the dreamer? Feed the drama and it will eat you. Feed the dreamer and it will nourish you. Your dreamer wolf is powerful. It is excited about creating a new reality. And best of all, it knows you are capable of this.

I know deep down that if I had kept feeding my drama wolf, I wouldn't be sitting on top of this beautiful building, next to a sapphire blue pool beneath the Scottsdale sun, surrounded by mountains, and writing this book. I wouldn't be praying for every person who reads my story and gets inspired to live a better story of their own!

You can only feed one wolf at a time. Which will you feed; which will you starve?

If you want to join me and feed your dreamer, let's look at some super practical ways to do this. We'll escape the drama triangle, live fully awake, and learn to hold the lines we draw for ourselves!

ESCAPE THE DRAMA TRIANGLE

Years ago someone close to us was battling addiction. Part of their rehabilitation was called family week, where the key people in the addict's life talk through everything that's been going on. Because addiction affects everyone, the entire family needs to heal together. There are hurt feelings expressed. Fingers of blame might be pointed. Trauma gets uncovered. These can be tough conversations to process.

One of the most powerful things I learned during family week was something called the Karpman drama triangle. The process places three roles at each point of a triangle: the persecutor, the rescuer, and the victim. And I was blown away because I saw how this simple little triangle perfectly describes how drama keeps popping up in relationships.

The victim acts like everyone and everything is out to get them. They are never to blame for negative things in their life; it's always someone else's fault. The victim blames but never takes responsibility. They are also dependent upon the other two roles. If the victim is not

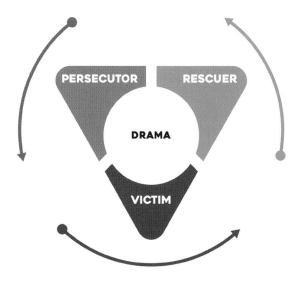

at the center of drama, they'll look for a persecutor or a rescuer to keep feeding their drama wolf.

The rescuer is always the hero—always needed. Deep down, they believe that no one can function without them. A rescuer feels guilty if they're not swooping in to save other people. And they are masters of making other people's problems their own. The main problems are that they enable the victims to keep avoiding responsibility and avoid their own problems by focusing on everyone but themselves.

The persecutor is the villain. They are the blamer, shamer, and finger wagger! They'll always see themselves as better than everyone else—and make darn sure you know it. They're great at controlling, manipulating, and oppressing other people.

Now, imagine a family where everyone is playing one of those parts. That's a recipe for drama that eventually boils over. And the truth is so many homes and communities are filled with people playing these parts. During family week, I started seeing how badly we were stuck orbiting Planet Drama.

As you read these, you might recognize some of those tendencies in yourself, your family, your friend group, coworkers, fellow church members, or all of the above! The question for all of us is: how in the heck do we get outta living like this?!

That's when we learned about the way to escape the drama triangle's toxic pull: the empowerment triangle.* It was created by the same psychologist who outlined the drama triangle. And in therapy, we learned that each drama role had a corresponding positive empowerment role.

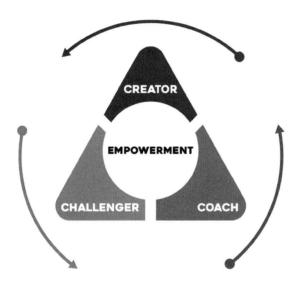

In the drama triangle, the victim blames the persecutor for their pain, and the rescuer steps in to save them. In the empowerment triangle, we find three new ways to exist together: the creator, the coach, and the challenger.

The creator is supercharged by their passion. They live to create a brighter future for themselves and those around them. Their focus isn't on how they're being persecuted (like the victim); they focus on what's possible.

The coach cares deeply about others. They love helping others create game plans for growth, seeing obstacles as opportunities. Instead of trying to rescue others by being the hero, they empower creators to be their own superhero.

The challenger thrives on personal growth in themselves and others. They're amazing at holding everyone accountable to be their best selves—not from a place of persecution, but of compassion. They're amazing encouragers and motivators.

Family week showed us that victims can become creators, rescuers can become coaches, and persecutors can become challengers. Together, we learned that inner healing for each of us is the first place to start—and that inner healing meant escaping the drama triangle.

Personally, I realized my habit of living as a rescuer. As an Enneagram Type 2, this came all too naturally to me! The idea of being an empowering coach perfectly aligned with my true, God-given purpose and identity. This process caused me to go to God. And the more I went to Him, the more He took me inward, showing me my true identity. This is where I found my own inner healing of restoration, hope, and joy.

Every month since that experience has been an exercise in holding the line against reentering the drama triangle. Let me tell you, drama is magnetic, but it's impossible to be completely healthy if you live there. Jumping into the drama pool to save someone only ends up with you both drowning. I've learned that living in the empowerment triangle and refusing to participate in drama is the only way I can truly serve humanity.

ARE YOU AWAKE?

Over the last decade, Doug and I have worked with literally tens of thousands of people. Over time we realized one of our first jobs as coaches is helping people wake up. So many live unconsciously, floating through life without intention. As we gently but firmly coached people to open their eyes and wipe the sleepiness away, we learned another psychological principle called the four stages of competence.*

Unconscious Incompetence	Conscious Incompetence
Someone doesn't know how to do something and doesn't realize they're incompetent.	*Someone doesn't know how to do something and realizes they're incompetent*
Conscious Competence	**Unconscious Competence**
Someone can do something but it requires significant effort to do so.	*Someone is so good at doing something it's become second nature*

SCAN ME

ˇ ORIGINALLY DEVELOPED BY NOEL BURCH

Competence is a skill in any area that can be learned. This is especially true in our mindset. When I went through this process, I realized that most people are addicted to the drama because they live an unconscious life. They simply don't know any other way. They get pulled into negativity and become dramaholics because they don't realize there is another choice.

As weird as talking about living outside of the drama zone as a skill might sound, it's absolutely true! It wasn't until then that I realized

I was an unconscious incompetent. I worked hard, and that gave me some initial success; but there was always a glass ceiling because I kept getting sucked back into old generational patterns.

When I learned to see, everything changed.

Author, coach, and dear friend of ours Dave Blanchard wrote an incredible book called *The Observer's Chair* that helped me wake up! In it, Dave talks about a unique ability we humans have called metacognition, the ability to be aware of our own thoughts. We can become an observer of our own life and decide how we'd like to think, act, and believe.

DAVE AND RAMONA BLANCHARD

SCAN ME

ˑ YOU CAN GET *THE OBSERVER'S CHAIR* HERE

When I started thinking about my thought life, I found broken beliefs and patterns—specifically letting drama fill my life. This was my process to becoming unconsciously competent, where refusing to engage in drama became second nature, a habit so ingrained it became automatic.

It all started by looking at the sandbox of drama and saying, "I refuse to play in here ever again!"

Is it time for you to make the same decision? Where are the sources of drama in your life? You? Your family, friends, coworkers, news media, or anyone in-between? You have to wake up and realize the drama wolf isn't serving you. In fact, it will never be satisfied until it's totally consumed you. When you go on an all-out drama detox, it'll feel awful. Just like an addict going through withdrawals to get to sobriety, dramaholics have to go cold turkey and hold the line.

I'm not going to pretend it's easy.

The hardest place to stay out of drama is in your family. If there is an ongoing cycle in your bloodline, you may need to seek professional help. Depending on how severe it is, you're not going to move through this without some great coaches, counselors, pastors, or spiritual advisors. It's going to take an army, so don't try to navigate it all by yourself.

What does it look like to find help? Sometimes it looks like checking into a treatment center, going to a marriage retreat, or seeing a family therapist. We need help getting the tools and resources to create boundaries and learn skills to move from the drama triangle to the empowerment triangle. And sometimes the only way is to seek professional help.

Creating a drama-free zone is chain-breaking work. It is hard, but so worth it because you can set generations after you free!

HOLDING THE LINE

Saying no drama is like drawing a line. I came to a point in my life where I had to realize drama was an actual addiction in my life. I had fed the drama wolf and now I had to starve it—and my oh my, does it ever howl!

When I finally made the decision to stop feeding drama, I felt like I'd discovered a superpower. It was like I could summon a magical force field like the girl from *The Incredibles*. Drama doesn't find me so much anymore because I stopped feeding the trolls!

In the Wood Family, we don't bring up the past and sling mud at each other. Because when we use past situations as weapons against one another, or as an excuse to complain, we're taking leaps backward. We're stumbling off the path. We're certainly not serving each other well. We have vowed to never play the blame-and-shame game.

Do we learn from our past together? Yes. Do we use it as an excuse to shame, blame, or manipulate? No!

As a family, we have committed to living above the drama zone. To honor this commitment, we've had to take drastic measures. What are you prepared to do to live drama-free?

Here are a few things we did.

We moved on from certain relationships. There were some friends with whom we stopped double dating, we quit going on vacations with, and whose Christmas parties we no longer attended. Honestly, this hurt some feelings and left situations feeling misunderstood. But their lives were drama zones—constantly trying to drag us into energy draining situations. It wasn't that they were bad people, it was about being around people who were committed to the same values, goals, and growth that we were.

We began attending a new church. Unfortunately, the church we had been attending didn't support or encourage our growth, holding us back and keeping us stuck in the past. Every week we left church disappointed and even more aggravated at the constant sarcasm and

cynicism. The truth was we had grown and changed, but nobody else had. It wasn't their fault we weren't fitting in any longer. It was time to move on.

We moved to a new city. Moving to a new city was our most drastic change, completely uprooting our lives! We also did it twice: once on a smaller scale, the second on a larger scale. Our first move was from Hillsboro to Tigard. While this was only about thirty miles, it signified a new season. We were committed to living conscious lives, totally awake, willing to do whatever it took to escape the drama zone. After this smaller shift, we eventually left Oregon completely for Arizona—and while we love our Oregonian family and friends, it was the decision that helped us rise above some patterns that were no longer serving us.

What do these moves look like in your life? Are you unhappy at work? Is your boss driving you crazy? Are your friends dragging you into their drama? Does your family ruin every holiday with bickering, gossip, and fighting? Is your church stuck in cynicism and complacency?

Don't let these situations keep you chained to your past self! These stressors leave us depleted to the point that all we can manage to do once we get home is sit down to watch TV. In fact, so many of us are living unconscious, unsatisfied lives because we spend every possible moment mindlessly consuming entertainment. On top of that, drama addicts and drains us, keeping us unfocused on our major areas of improvement and stuck in small-mindedness. We're trapped in the comparison game, judging our lives by those of others.

It's time to get out!

Find the areas of your life that are dragging you down. Find the drag and you will uncover the drama. Identify these issues and refuse to participate in it. Get ready, though. I guarantee you that the wrong people in your life will misunderstand your newfound boundaries. You're going to piss some people off on this new adventure, but it's going to be so worth it! In fact, eventually these people will turn around and applaud you. It won't happen right away, but your best yes will become a breakthrough for others.

Now is the time to make the change! Direct your energy toward creation, not commiseration. Stop spending your mental bandwidth on junk. Say no to drama and actively work to get away from every source of it in your life.

As you do, remember, you can climb every ladder of success in life; yet no matter how much you accomplish, you can always get drawn back into drama. It's a constant force that will try and drag you down. You're never beyond it. And in my life, I have learned to be conscious of my decisions surrounding potential drama.

Where focus goes, energy flows. I draw a line in the sand where I will put zero energy into drama. And I hold it!

Ultimately, I do this for far more than my own happiness—I do it for the generations to come. Fear Kicker, I invite you to do the same. Ditch the drama and experience incredible momentum toward a bright future, filled with abundance, blessing, and impact.

Deuteronomy 7:9

"Know therefore that the Lord your God is God; he is the faithful God, keeping his covenant of love to a thousand generations of those who love him and keep his commandments."

CHAPTER 8

REMNANT GENERATIONAL BLESSINGS

Do you remember when the carnival rolled into your town when you were a kid?

Every time your parents drove by it, the towering Ferris wheels, roaring roller coasters, and clouds of cotton candy captured all your attention. You begged and pleaded to go tonight . . . or tomorrow night . . . or any night before they packed up and moved on. The years you did get to go were unforgettable. Popcorn, sticky fingers, and bursts of color were everywhere.

Carnivals are a kid's dream, right?

Now imagine if your grandparents owned the carnival and you got to play every game, try every ride, and stuff your face with candy for free. That was our life growing up. My grandparents were carneys. To me and my sisters, this could not have been any cooler!

Every year they would get the latest and greatest rides that we and our friends got to enjoy until our stomachs couldn't handle it anymore. I remember one year the big thing everyone talked about

was the Gravitron. It was a disc ringed with lights that looked like a spaceship. When you climbed in, everyone leaned against boards on tracks against the wall. Slowly at first, the disc would spin, then faster and faster until the force pinned you against the board, which slid up and down! We were absolutely addicted to this ride and spent hours on it, in between cotton candy breaks, of course.

Those fun, unforgettable experiences are wonderful to reflect on. However, today, those memories mean more to me than nostalgic happiness. Along with warm fuzzies, they leave me in awe at what God does through generations of His people. My grandparents toured the entire country, bringing joy and laughter to towns big and small.

In the summer of 2019, Doug and I took our family on a tour across the United States, bringing hope and encouragement in twenty-five different cities. We empowered people to live on purpose by creating abundance in their lives, families, and finances.*

I know this drive to help people across the country create momentum in their lives directly ties back to my grandparents. They traveled, working tirelessly to set up and tear down an entire carnival in city after city. During the times I traveled with them to help, they taught me grit, work ethic, and a love for new places. They also prayed over my life and future. They asked God to bless me and my siblings, and they asked that we would believe Jesus was who He said He was, trusting everything we have to Him.

Those prayers (and many more) are being answered in my life today. We walk in supernatural blessing that started decades ago. I believe many of you do as well.

There are dreams and destinies within you prayed from generations ago. Right now, you are the answer to that prayer. Your life is bigger than you. It stretches back decades to your grandparents, great-grandparents, and beyond.

Blessing goes back generations and flows forward into your legacy. Your prayers for God's favor and anointing on your children, your

---

* I share the full story of that wild tour in chapter 17!

proclamations for victory over generational addiction cycles, your dreams of abundance for your current or future grandchildren, great-grandchildren, and beyond . . . You may never see those prayers, proclamations, or dreams fulfilled in your time on this earth. But that's the kind of vision that changes nations.

Fear Kickers, here is the path for accepting and passing on generational blessing: accept what you've received with gratitude and partner with God to break bondage going forward.

We dream beyond ourselves. We imagine bigger things than we could accomplish in a single lifetime. We believe greater things are yet to come in future generations. Today, I know I'm living in some of the dreams that were birthed—but unrealized—in my parents and grandparents.

The same is true for you and will be true for forthcoming generations. But we've got some work to do to help them on their way.

CLEAR THE PATH

Jesus had a cousin named John. Most people know him as John the Baptist. He lived in the desert, dressed in camel's hair, and ate locusts and wild honey. Today he would be quite the sight—but back then people understood that he was dressed in traditional prophet's gear and ate a strict diet according to religious purity laws. God had an important job for John to do. But it started about seven hundred years before he was born.

Isaiah was a prophet who wrote about John centuries before he lived, describing John as "A voice of one calling: 'In the wilderness prepare the way for the LORD; make straight in the desert a highway for our God'" (Isaiah 40:3). John's job was to clear the way for Jesus to enter the scene. He had to contend with generational junk the people held onto. He was like a signpost pointing people to Jesus, preparing their hearts and minds for a new reality to come rushing in!

He was to clear a path and break up some old thought patterns that would have made people miss the blessing of eternal life God sent to their doorstep. Today we have a similar job. We're all little John the Baptists, clearing paths for future generations to walk in God's purposes for them.

We break bondage and pass on what's good. Doug and I often call these bondages generational beasts. They're the demons that nipped at your grandparent's heels. The broken patterns that held your parents. The addiction cycles trying to take you out.

However, Fear Kickers are the people who draw a line and declare: this is where it stops. Those beasts don't run in our family any longer, they've run out! We don't pass on beasts; we pass down blessings. For us, this took a serious survey of what beasts tried to run wild in our families. We had to decide what our family tree was going to look like. And we realized the stakes were high because this wasn't about us; it was about future generations.

KATELYN

We began to look fifty and a hundred years ahead, dreaming what would happen if we broke cycles of food and sugar addiction, substance abuse, pornography use, fear of people's opinions, debt and financial struggle, limiting beliefs, and more! Our job was to break down stronghold after stronghold, clearing the path for family members who haven't even been born yet.

I've caught glimpses of this in my life. When I was a girl, I dreamed of being a dancer. I imagined myself as a ballerina, leaping gracefully through the air, twirling with perfect balance in front of clapping audiences. Only, my parents couldn't afford the lessons, recitals, travel, and more that it took to become a dancer.

Fast forward to one night, sitting in a packed audience with my husband Doug, watching our daughter Katelyn dance. She's amazing, every bit as graceful as I had dreamed, fully capable of mesmerizing an audience. Seeing her flourish like this made me smile at God, because my daughter was living a dream that had been placed on my heart. In that moment, I experienced joy and gratitude at this incredible blessing.

What about you? What dreams or visions do you have for future generations? And more importantly, what blessing will you pass on, and what bondage will you break? If you don't deal with your bondage, the next generation will have to deal with it.

BORN TO BREAK CHAINS

Bondage means to be held captive. You're tied up, held back, and kept from moving where you want in life. I believe we were born to break chains and slay those generational beasts. I've found three powerful ways to do it: call out your beasts, change the patterns, and model freedom.

First, we call out our beasts. It's hard to fight an enemy you either don't see or won't acknowledge. What beasts keep creeping around in your family? Have you made peace with bondage that it's time to break? We *all* have beasts in our families—it's time to call them out!

Second, we change the patterns. Next time you go to the zoo, pay attention to the wolves. You'll notice circular trails around the edges of their enclosure. They run in predictable patterns, circling in the same path every time. Our generational beasts are often the same way. They strike at us in the same places, situations, and circumstances. Where do your beasts rear their heads? How can you break that pattern and interrupt it?

For our family, this has meant changing churches, limiting time with certain family and friends, and even moving to a new state! I don't know what it will look like for you. It may be smaller than our work to change those patterns—or it may be even bigger. All I know is that generational beasts, once called out, can be spotted. They pounce in predictable places. It's our job to change those patterns!

Before moving on, I do also want to say there are real traumas and addictions that go too deep for us to resolve on our own. I fully acknowledge that we need help; my family sure did. Part of your fight is to reach out to the right people and resources, like coaches, pastors, or trauma therapists to help.

Third, we model freedom! What does it look like to live free of these generational beasts? Beliefs and behaviors are caught as much as they're taught. It's not enough to talk about freedom; we have to walk in freedom. Our kids watch us. What does it look like to live free from fear, debt, pornography, substance addictions, and more?

This goes even further. While we do it for our families, the church is supposed to do this for the world. God's people are called to be a light to all nations; a city set on a hill that can't be hidden.* Are we modeling hope, abundance, love, godly father- and motherhood, generosity, grace, self-control, kindness, faithfulness, integrity, and more?

I believe this is more important today than in any previous generation because the stakes are higher than they've ever been.

THE NEW GREATEST GENERATION

In recent years, Doug and I began to travel the world annually. In 2017 we spent months in Europe and Israel with our entire family, and we've visited many other countries since. Our travels have given us a global perspective—and we started to realize that our kids weren't being as well-prepared by the school system for the world we live in as they could be. We don't fault any of our public or private schools. But we did want an alternative way for our kids to learn and be prepared as entrepreneurial leaders and global citizens. We wanted them to see the massive challenges people face and understand how to innovate and solve them. This meant they'd need to

DOUG & I WITH ANGIE

understand technology, business, and entrepreneurship.

* Check out Isaiah 42:6; Isaiah 49:6; Isaiah 52:10; Isaiah 60:3; John 8:12; Acts 13:47; Acts 26:23; Matthew 5:14.

VALOR CREW

We couldn't find what we were looking for until we met Angie Taylor - a world-changing, out-of-the-box educator who shared our heart. Together, we co-founded Valor Global Online (the school I talked about in Chapter 2). I am so passionate about this school because I believe our children are the new greatest generation. They are the people who can scale blessing around the world like no other generation in history! Their voices can be heard instantly on every continent.

We want them to understand their place and harness that power. To raise a generation of chain-breakers, we are drowning out death speech with life talk. Where culture calls them addicted to screens, we help them see they are digital natives. Where culture calls them lazy, we help them see how to apply the right amount of effort in the best places. Where culture calls them selfish, we help them see how to live generously by connecting them with causes they care deeply about.

We want kids to break out of the boxes they've been stuck in. Our kids, and every generation after, need to see their identity outside of career tracks, titles, and promotions. They need to own who they are

AMAYA IN KENYA ON A TRIP WITH VALOR

in Jesus and live out their God-given purpose. While Valor began as solution for our family's need, it is quickly becoming a movement that will ripple into the coming generations.

Our message is that today's youth are the greatest generation to ever live on this planet. There has never been a time on earth to bring the creative genius of heaven into reality like we live in now.

WHOEVER'S READING THIS:

YOU ARE SPECIAL! YOU HAVE POTENTIAL!

YOU CAN CHANGE THE WORLD!

FEAR KICKER, YOU'RE APPOINTED,

ANOINTED, AND HAVE WHAT IT TAKES.

If you feel that fight in you and you want to contend against the generational beasts and lies trying to take us down, it's because it's your time to rise up. Former generations couldn't quite kick some of these beasts—but we can.

THE PAIN OF CHANGE IS WORTH IT

I'm excited for you and your opportunity to create change and build a legacy of impact. However, I'm also aware that it is going to take work. Serious work. And along with hard work comes some pain. You will be sore and develop some calluses. Contending against generational beasts might tick some people off—especially in your family. Your growth will threaten some people. I'm not promising you it will be easy, but I do promise it will be worth it.

There was a moment on our Massive Momentum tour I'll never forget. Doug and I had just finished speaking for the night. Our favorite thing to do afterward was open up the mic for questions from the audience. The questions were always amazing, as people were grappling with how to create positive momentum in their lives. But I'll never forget this one.

A woman stood up, taking the microphone. She described how deeply she loved her family and friends, but they didn't understand the positive lifestyle changes she was making. In reality, they weren't happy with the way she was contending with their generational beasts! Her heart wanted to break free from some addiction cycles that she didn't want her children to contend with.

Exasperated, she asked, "Is it really gonna be worth it to contend and be a chain-breaker?"

The audience was silent; everyone leaned in. This was the question on everyone's heart. There is pain in breaking generational chains. It's confusing and hard. Every eye looked at me echoing the same question. "Thea, is it *really* worth it?"

I had answered questions like this a million times. But instantly, like a download from heaven, a new answer popped into my head that I had never shared before.

I said, "Hi, I am Sophia. I am your great-great-granddaughter. I just want you to know that because you contended against obesity, food addiction, small thinking, and fear, I'm living my dreams, walking in uncommon blessing, and making a massive impact on the world around me. Thank you for setting our bloodline free."

Everyone sat still, contemplating a message of gratitude from their own future great-great-grandchildren. Honestly, this was one of the most powerful moments on the whole tour. It connected us all with the impact our actions *today* have on a thousand *tomorrows*.

What about your future generations? What will they thank you for? What bondage are you breaking to set them free? What beasts are you slaying for them? What territory are you taking back? What abundance, dreams, and blessings are you creating for them to walk in?

Every time we kick fear, it's like we plant a tree. At first, it doesn't seem like much. But day after day, month after month, year after year, that tree grows. Over time, it buds and produces fruit. The branches mature, the leaves expand, and there is shade. And of course, there are thousands of seeds for a forest's worth of trees to come.

Future generations will sit beneath the shade of every tree you plant today. They will eat and share the fruit of your work. And they will find the strength to plant trees of their own. My friend, you aren't planting a garden, you're starting a forest. It begins with a single seed. Though it starts small, oh how grateful they will be.

You were made for such a time as this—because generations are counting on you to show up, play big, and kick fear in the face!

Esther 4:14

"For if you remain silent at this time, relief and
deliverance for the Jews will arise from another place,
but you and your father's family will perish. And who
knows but that you have come to your royal position for
such a time as this?"

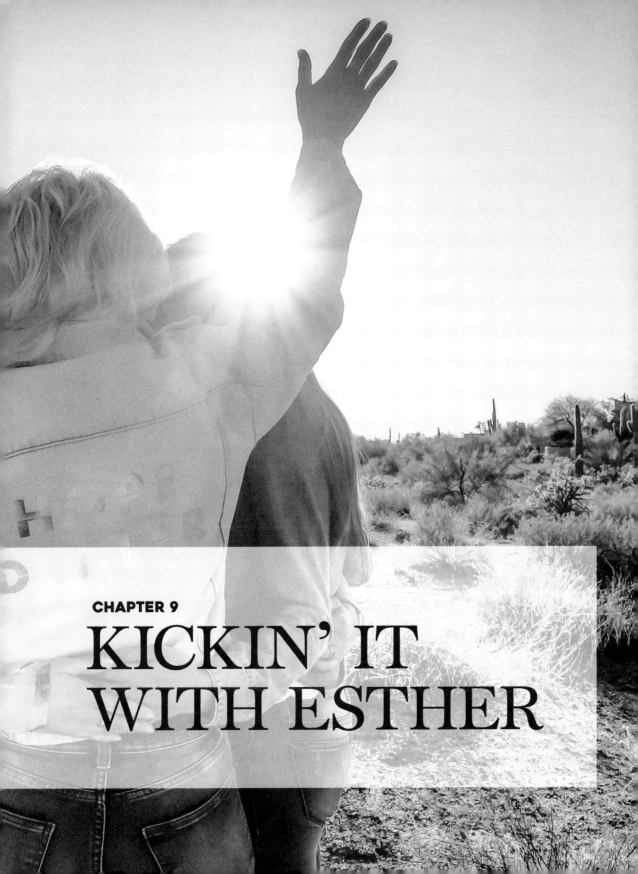

CHAPTER 9

KICKIN' IT WITH ESTHER

KICKIN' IT WITH ESTHER

Thousands of years ago, a young woman was prepared to risk her life by walking into the presence of the world's most powerful king. It was a crime to approach this king without an invitation. The punishment? Death. But still this girl was ready to march straight into the throne room, willing to give it all for the purpose God had placed on her life.

Of course I'm talking about Esther, whose story is in the book of Esther in the Old Testament. I have constantly returned to her story for inspiration for years. Because when my life feels overwhelming and I could easily be paralyzed by fear, I can look at her standing brave, kicking fear in the face, and taking action even when she was scared.

What's remarkable is that Esther probably felt totally out of place, wondering why on earth God put her in this position. You see, as a Jewish woman, she wasn't in an environment that embraced or even tolerated her. Her situation must have felt impossible. But in the face of a death sentence, she said, "If I die, I die."

Here's how she got to that defining moment and how we can follow her lead every single day. I believe you were born at exactly the right time, in precisely the right place, and have arrived where you are today for a reason—just like she did. What you do today matters because you were born for such a time as this.

FOR SUCH A TIME AS THIS

Esther lived in a city called Susa, the capital of the wealthy and powerful Persian empire, where a small group of Jews did their best to remain faithful. They had been exiled, ripped from their homes over a hundred years before. And things were getting even worse.

Esther's uncle, a man named Mordecai, took her in after her parents had died. They lived a quiet life until King Xerxes ditched his wife, Queen Vashti, after she refused to obey one of his drunken orders. The king sent servants throughout the city to find him a woman worthy of replacing Vashti as queen.

As it turned out, Esther was an absolute bombshell. She was graceful, gorgeous, and totally captivating. So, the king's servants scooped her up and took her to the palace to put her in the running to become the new Queen of Persia. While she did her best to remain true to her faith, her Uncle Mordecai warned her to keep her Jewish heritage a secret—which she did.

What was crazy is that these women weren't immediately placed into a beauty pageant, walking the runway to impress the king. They began a year-long process of intense preparation! Over the coming months, God poured out His favor out on her in extreme abundance.

When the king saw her, he was immediately entranced by her overwhelming beauty and kindness and placed the crown on her head. For Esther, life seemed to have just reached its pinnacle. While this sounds like the setup to this year's breakout Hallmark movie, it took a grittier turn.

Shortly after she became queen, an advisor to the king named Haman became enraged at her Uncle Mordecai. Haman had an ego larger than the kingdom of Persia itself and required everyone to bow to him in the streets. But Mordecai refused to bow. He stood defiantly, saying he only bowed his head to Jehovah, the God of his fathers. This infuriated Haman. He saw red and decided it wasn't enough to punish Mordecai alone with death. He wanted to exterminate his whole people group—the Jews.

Haman came before King Xerxes with lies and accusations against the Jews. He then convinced Xerxes to pass a law that all Jews—men, women, and children—would be put to death in one year. Not only would the Jews be put to death, but anyone who killed a Jew could take possession of their property. This was going to be genocide.

When Mordecai heard this, he tore his robe and wept bitterly at the city gate. Everyone going in and out saw him like this. Esther sent a servant to see what was wrong with her uncle. Mordecai replied telling her about the coming genocide, begging her to go before the king to plead for the lives of the Jewish people. When Esther heard this, she was terrified for her people, but as I said, to go before the king without an invitation meant death.

Esther had every reason to say no. After all, couldn't she fly under the radar without being outed as a Jew? Couldn't she cozy up to the king for protection? There had to be a way to save herself. However, her uncle encouraged her with these words: "If you don't speak up now, we will somehow get help, but you and your family will be killed. It could be that you were made queen for a time like this" (Esther 4:14).

Esther found her courage and went straight to her energy source. She replied, "Go, gather all the Jews to be found in Susa, and hold a fast on my behalf, and do not eat or drink for three days, night or day. I and my young women will also fast as you do. Then I will go to the king, though it is against the law, and if I perish, I perish" (Esther 4:16).

I love this part of the story because Esther's first thought is, "I'm gonna grab my gang of girls to fast and pray with me. Uncle Mordecai, you do the same." She knew that the true battle was not against flesh and blood, but against the powers and principalities of this dark world. And she also knew it was time to get her beehive community buzzing!

Esther was fighting an uphill battle against a culture that didn't want to take just her out, but also her entire bloodline. Generations upon generations were about to be wiped out.

She contended against the rules in approaching the king, an evil leader who plotted to kill her entire people. And she already lived in an incredibly controlling culture where women were expected to sit down and be quiet. In fact, after Queen Vashti had been replaced because she didn't come to King Xerxes exactly when he summoned her, the king drafted a letter to his entire empire saying that men should be in charge over their children and wives. It's hard for us to imagine how many cultural expectations Esther was swimming against by being obedient to God. Culture tries to tell you that you're only allowed to do so many things, that you're only permitted to go as far as your predetermined box allows you to.

RISE UP

So often, who we are called to be and what we are called to do is on the other side of kicking down tradition and cultural norms. You can either succumb to culture, or you can create culture. You could say, "Well, people in my family got divorced; I probably will too . . ." No! You can reject the story thrown on you. God is writing a new story with your life! You're a chain-breaker, not a chain-wearer.

In order to kick fear in the face you're gonna have to rise up against bondage and fear. You have to rise against the resentment, lies, and limiting beliefs holding you back. Esther didn't do it alone, and we shouldn't either. When I did this in my own life, I found my tribe. I didn't have people who were living this way in my immediate circle, so I brought my friends together like Esther and contended in the spiritual realm before I even started to move in the natural. We contended forward together. I rallied my prayer partners, invited my fellow Fear Kickers, and brought them into my life. "Can you pray today and stand in the gap with me for my marriage, my mind, my decisions . . . ?"

Can you pray today and stand in the gap with me . . .

I didn't fight my battles alone, and you shouldn't either. We are better together—especially in the most intense situations. Esther believed this and acted on it, and so do Fear Kickers. And as Jesus would say hundreds of years later in Matthew 18:20, "For where two or three gather in my name, there am I with them." He stands with us in our unity.

GOD'S TIMING

Kicking fear in the face means, you know, you're going to do some things afraid! Esther's decision also shows us this. She went before the king to plead for her people before she was ready. She felt like she could have used more time, but she placed her faith in the Lord that He would take her faith as the extra boost she needed in her weakness. Sometimes you won't feel ready to do what has to be done, but NOW is the time.

You were born for such a time as this.

Fear tells you that you need more money. Culture tells you that you need a new job. Your insecurity screams that you need to lose more weight. Your family tradition demands that you need to graduate college first. *But the true king is calling!* The time isn't tomorrow—the time is now. We are tempted to slam on the brakes and say, "Whoa, I need to get it together and know exactly what the path forward looks like . . ." But we have to trust God's timing and preparation for us. When we move ahead, even when we don't see beyond the next step, we activate our inner Esthers by pulling tomorrow into today.

HERE'S ONE OF THE SECRETS TO THIS: DO THE LITTLE THINGS TODAY TO PREPARE YOURSELF FOR THE BIG THINGS TOMORROW.

Guys, go to the barber and put on some cologne! Ladies, instead of stretchy pants put on your skinny jeans! Get dressed for the day. Put on your kickin' it heels! Show up as your best, most authentic self every day. When God asks you to do the bigger things, you will have already flexed that obedience muscle. You'll be fit for the challenge because the Holy Spirit has been prepping you for massive action for such a time as this.

We're going to talk a lot more about him in chapter 13, but David's life is an amazing example of this. Before he ever fought Goliath, he battled lions and bears by hand. (Real talk, lions and bears still sound pretty huge to me!) Partner with God in the little things, and when the big things come, you'll be ready. His strength is made perfect in our weakness.

HOW TO MOVE FORWARD

I love what bestselling author and pastor Mark Batterson says about moving forward. Basically, many people are stuck in a cycle of seeing their fears as giant obstacles, too big to move, too wide to navigate around. Mark encourages us that instead of putting those fears (obstacles) between us and God, let's put God between us and our fears. Wow—what a thought, right?

I believe that one of the main ways God steps into our situations is through divine community. If you don't have your crew, create it. Believe that God is divinely bringing the right people in place around you, and you will find your obstacle-busting tribe. It might be small, like Daniel's when he was with Shadrad, Mechak, and Abednego in Babylon. It might be huge, like Esther's nearly entire nation praying and contending alongside her. Regardless, you need one.

I WANT YOU TO EXPAND YOUR

UNDERSTANDING OF WHAT A TRIBE IS.

I see so many people make the mistake of only bringing people their same age into their beehive. Esther, on the other hand, engaged everyone that God put in her life, regardless of age. Generationally,

we need the fifty-, sixty-, and seventy-year-olds to partner with ten-, fifteen-, and twenty-year-olds. Let's take a cue from Esther by finding these older, wiser Fear Kickers and partnering with their experience to bring the full force of community against our fears.

The incredible thing about her fellow prayer warriors is that they weren't powerful and prestigious. They were the captives, the most powerless ones, condemned to die! The power of this community was in their shared heart, mind, and vision for the future. These are the people to run with and who will work to bring tomorrow into today.

HERO FOR THE AGES

Esther's community helped her become a hero for the ages. She was also extremely clever. She put on her finest eye-catching clothes and stood in front the king's quarters, where he sat on his throne. When he saw Esther, he pointed his golden scepter at her, allowing her to

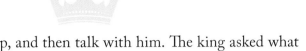

approach, touch its tip, and then talk with him. The king asked what she wanted, promising up to half of his kingdom.

She asked simply, "Will you and Haman come to a feast I'm preparing in your honor?" The king was thrilled, telling Haman to come along. Then at this private feast, the king asked her again, "What do you want?" She invited the pair to another feast the next evening.

Haman left full of confidence and self-importance, thinking he was really something special. All he could think about was how great he was and how worthless Mordecai was. He bragged about his power to his wife, Zeresh, and to all his friends. But as he talked about his hatred for Mordecai, they came up with an idea, saying, "Build a towering gallows to hang him."

Haman smiled, quite happy with their scheme. He had the gallows constructed and planned to tell the king to hang Mordecai. Haman went to bed thinking he'd won. But that night, King Xerxes couldn't sleep. He ordered his servants to get a record book called *The Book of Memorable Deeds* and read it to him. It was like a highlight reel of all the awesome things people had done in the kingdom.

It just so happened one of the memorable deeds that got read was about Mordecai and how he had once bravely broken up a plot to kill the king. Mordecai had saved King Xerxes's life! So he asked what honor had been given to him as a reward. The servants shrugged and said, "Nothing . . ."

Here's where it gets *really* good. While King Xerxes works through all this, Haman shows up to tell him to have Mordecai hanged on his freshly built gallows. But King Xerxes asks Haman an interesting question: "What should I do to honor someone very important to me?"

Automatically, Haman thought the king was talking about himself. So he said, "Put royal robes on him that you yourself have worn, put him on a horse you've ridden, and let him be paraded around with one of your crowns on his head." I can see Haman's hungry expression now—licking his lips, just ready to get decked out in kingly gear.

Then King Xerxes delivered the news. "Go as fast as you can, grab the robes, the horse, and the crown, and give them to Mordecai the Jew, who's at the gate." And who had to deliver them? Haman! He did what he was told and marched Mordecai around the city, telling everyone how much the king loved and honored him. This sent him into a rage . . . But when he returned, it was time for the second feast.

The king asked Esther again what she wanted. She shared the truth about Haman's plot to have the Jews killed. And for this treachery and evil, Haman was hanged on the very gallows he'd built for Mordecai. The king also wrote a new law that the Jews could defend themselves against any attackers—and they kicked some serious booty!

Esther had become queen, and Mordecai, the second most powerful man in the country just after the king. He worked hard to take care of his people, the very community that joined with Esther to pray and fast when everything seemed lost.

Instead of death, God brought life. Instead of injustice, God brought justice. Instead of fear, God rewarded faith. Esther was born for such a time as this and became a hero. Over the years, Esther has helped me fight from a place of victory and proclaim God's goodness. I know God is working all things together for my good. I'm gonna do my part. I'm gonna say yes. I'm gonna show up. I will do the hard things because I know that I, too, have been born for such a time as this.

Kicking fear in the face will be hard. It will even feel overwhelming at times. But the reward far outweighs the difficulty. Today, kick it with Esther to kick fear in the face. I believe there are big things ahead for you and the generations that will be impacted after you. And like Esther's life shows, it's going to take some major shifts, which is what we're tackling next.

Isaiah 43:19

"See, I am doing a new thing! Now it springs up; do you not perceive it? I am making a way in the wilderness and streams in the wasteland."

CHAPTER 10

SHIFT HAPPENS

Doug and I were in our late teens, falling in love like crazy. We were on fire for Jesus and each other, with hearts thrown wide open for God's will. Honestly, I was prepared to go anywhere and do anything for His Kingdom.

I had thrown myself wholeheartedly into Masters Commission straight out of high school, preparing for a life of ministry and changing the world for Jesus. From a young age, I'd felt a huge call in my life to do big things for God, and this was the launching pad. As long as I was spending time in His presence and doing His work, I was fulfilled and happy. So, when I met Doug, and saw his passion for God and natural leadership, I was drawn to him like a magnet. We grew side by side in our love for, and knowledge of, God.

This was a beautiful season.

At this time in my faith journey, I had developed a passion for street ministry. I remember walking down the sweltering streets of Phoenix, feeling God's overwhelming love for broken people. The simple act of approaching someone slumped against the side of a building, with no intention except to be Jesus to them, was everything to me. Time after time, I learned that a single Spirit-filled prayer can release Holy Spirit miracles.

Pain points were becoming purpose points. God was redirecting people and healing them in unbelievable ways. I had fallen deeply in love with the process of partnering with God to lift people out of depression and hopelessness and to fill them instead with new life.

At the end of our first year in Masters Commission, Doug went back to Oregon, and I went back to Iowa. We both took our passion home with us, completely on the same wavelength. We kept God as the focal point of our relationship, and we developed our partnership despite the miles separating us. The summer before I was going to go back to ministry school, Doug invited me to Oregon. But not just for a little visit . . . This is where things got *real!*

He invited me to live with his grandma so we could really pursue a relationship toward marriage. At nineteen I was faced with the decision to leave all I had ever known for a man I loved or to stay comfortable in my hometown and go back to my second year of Masters Commission.

You know those moments where you have an intuitive sense that your entire future is balanced on one decision? This was one of those times. So, I went to my dad for advice on this difficult decision.

I'll never forget standing in our kitchen together. Nervous and sweaty-palmed, I shared what was on my heart: the opportunity to go to Oregon to see where Doug's and my relationship could go. I didn't feel judgment or skepticism from my dad. Instead, I felt nothing but love and concern.

He listened then said simply, "I think you're supposed to go to Oregon."

In a single sentence, my future opened up. His blessing confirmed my move and future life with Doug. However, this meant a massive shift was about to take place. Iowa and Oregon might be in the same country, but they are very different places. I was about to pack up, leave everything I'd known, and travel three thousand miles to live with my boyfriend's grandma—that wasn't crazy, right?!

MY DAD GIVING ME AWAY ON MY WEDDING DAY

Growing up, I had been pretty sheltered, as my life revolved around my small family, church, and school. I was coming off my first year at Masters Commission, which had at least given me some broader life experience. But I was completely unprepared for the feelings that welled up in me when I pulled into Doug's grandma's driveway. Everything I owned was packed into my car—I was uprooting my entire life.

It smacked me square in the face, and I remember saying to myself: "I'm moving into a house with a seventy-year-old I don't even know."

This is the first time I realized shift happens—and when it does, we have a decision to embrace or resist it. There are transitions in life that don't allow us to go halfway. While there are twenty years between that driveway moment and sitting on top of a beautiful building in downtown Scottsdale writing this book, I realize I pushed a domino that day. This shift caused a chain reaction that would run through my life. While I could share dozens of them, there have been four shifts that were hard, scary, and unnerving, which I'm so happy I made.

I'm sure you've made massive shifts in your life as well. I also know there are more ahead of you. And what you decide to do in those moments makes or breaks the abundant future ahead of you. For me, the first shift reframed the way I saw myself, my role in the world, and every choice I had to make.

SHIFT #1: FROM "ME" TO "WE"

To put it lightly, I did not realize how much Doug's and my relationship would change the closer we got to marriage. When we walked down the aisle and took each other's hands under the sight of God, I had no clue how much shifting would happen on the other side of "to have and to hold from this day forward." We gazed at each other, tears in our eyes, and said our honest "I do's." Our family and friends cheered us on as we kissed and marched out as man and wife! But it didn't take long for my shift into wifehood to look nothing like I had imagined it to be.

We had burned the bridges to the Masters Commission, ministry, and my old hometown; so I threw myself into our relationship. I was all in—but that ministry-filled Kingdom life I'd prepared for wasn't coming to pass. Instead, we committed ourselves to Doug's family business in furniture sales, and his parents helped to set us up in the best part of town. The building we chose required a ten-year lease at $20,000 per month.

Doug signed on the dotted line. Both of us were strong and ready to build a future, but as we worked together, cracks started to spiderweb in our marriage. It didn't take long for the lease to shift from excitement to burden.

Doug has always been a strong leader, and I've always been equally strong and independent. So in working together, it didn't take long for friction to start throwing sparks. Simple conversations turned into arguments. Every day I felt more like an employee and less like a wife and partner. The financial pressures kept piling up on Doug, and our marriage started to suffer.

I caught myself thinking, *This isn't what I signed up for.* I want to be a wife, mother, and partner, not an employee who's always on the clock.

I wanted to take back control of my story, and I started thinking that if I could just become a mom, everything would make more sense. This would give me a place and purpose I didn't have. We talked about children, but he didn't feel like we were financially ready for that responsibility. This drove the wedge between us even deeper.

Then things got even worse. I remember the terrorist attacks on September 11, 2001 rocking the world and our marriage at the same time. Our finances crumbled as the retail industry bottomed out. Our furniture business felt like a deflated balloon, causing stress to pile onto Doug even higher. Debts piled up and the lease was due every month, but the money just wasn't there. Our arguments intensified. And we could both see the writing on the wall. If we didn't change, we weren't going to make it.

I broke away from the family business, taking a retail job at Victoria's Secret. We settled into an uneasy rhythm, still growing further apart. The unspoken rule in our marriage became "You have your life, I have mine." We passed each other like ships in the night. Slowly, we morphed from partners to roommates. With the stress and emotional issues, we both gained weight at an alarming rate. We buried our feelings and frustrations in food. Life passed by, leaving us numb and trying to ignore the elephant in the room.

Unfortunately, our marriage started to mirror the relationships of those around us. We allowed our friends at that time to muddy the waters of morality. A friend invited me out to her bachelorette party, and I was grateful for a chance to let my hair down and tune things out. That night we hit bar after bar as the moon climbed higher into the sky, and when the shots started flowing freely, I was transported back to the little girl in Germany. God was tapping me on my shoulder calling me out of that darkness, and I knew I was wandering off the path to greater destiny. Our friends started getting married, throwing cycles of bachelor and bachelorette parties. With each party I felt my light slipping away. We were frogs slowly simmering in a kettle we should never have climbed into.

Our community didn't share our values, and we weren't staying plugged into a church. Week after week, we put in seventy hours at work, leaving us with little energy for each other. I wanted to live a life that changed the world, but how could I when my own world felt like a dying fire?

The furniture business was facing a major financial crunch, and money stress crushed Doug. If you've ever experienced financial stress, you know how all-consuming it is. That furniture store lease was like a boulder hanging over Doug's head, always threatening to crash down on us. Even worse, it was a family business, and no one wants to fail their family.

We started married life in a beautiful apartment in a nice area of town, but when money got tight, we moved into a small one-bedroom place across the street from the store. I couldn't help but stare up at the black ceiling from my bed and wonder where our life was headed. The only ray of hope I could see was having a baby. If only we had a baby and I became a mom, everything would be better.

But things would have to get worse before they got better. The stress pulled us further apart. I isolated and so did he. This is when Doug slipped into his pornography addiction, and I joined in with him in an effort to find intimacy again. We crossed moral boundaries that we swore we would never cross, and I felt broken. Our fights grew even more bitter. My desire for a baby, the stress of his business, and the growing distance between us all boiled over into a full-on blowout between us.

This was not what I had signed up for. When the heat of our argument was in full force, I turned my back to him and went straight for my suitcase. I felt like packing up my stuff and our dog and heading back to Iowa when Doug was at work the next day.

The shift from "me" to "we" seemed like a nightmare instead of a honeymoon.

SHIFT #2: TAKING RESPONSIBILITY AND REJECTING BLAME

With nowhere left to turn to I made a last desperate call to Doug's mom. She showered me with love and support by offering to pay for counseling. But I wanted to scream at the sky, "How did I get here?!"

With that question echoing in my mind, I accepted the help, starting intensive private counseling sessions. Through professional therapy I saw the patterns in myself that had to change for our marriage to heal.

I had formed an identity as Thea the Puritan. That identity was encouraged and solidified by my upbringing. Anytime I pushed the boundaries in the slightest I was severely reprimanded. There was never freedom to explore myself and my world because I was caught in the rigid structure of religious culture. I grew up believing that if I was good, God and I were on good terms. He loved me when I was a good girl doing the good things I was supposed to do. But if I was bad, God was an angry dad in the sky just waiting to stomp me under His shoe when I stepped out of line. I wanted so badly to be everything that my dad wanted me to be, and I used that same people-pleasing attitude toward God.

Growing up, I had romanticized the perfect biblical marriage that I would someday have with the man of my dreams. In fact, while dating, Doug and I decided to not even kiss each other for the last two months to make sure that we stayed pure. I was trying to learn what intimacy was in marriage; but I had protected my sexuality so closely that when it came time to express it in a marriage context, I didn't know how to handle what came next.

I'd never even had a conversation about sex. In the church world, sex was a dirty topic that a good Christian girl wouldn't want to discuss. Instead of the beautiful, amazing, God-created gift that it is, it was off-limits, like a necessary evil to be ignored.

This is when I embraced the shift from "me" to "we" and worked to show up differently in our marriage. I formed a loving relationship with my body, creating healthier eating habits. Counseling had shown me that I had to take responsibility for what I could change, but also that I couldn't accept the whole fault on myself.

From that point on I was on a mission to contend for the life I knew we were called to lead. Doug was still under intense stress in the furniture business, so I committed to show up as his partner every single day. At night, I would pray for him and anoint his feet with oil. That might sound like the weirdest thing ever, but in the Old Testament, Isaiah 21:5 told the military officers at that time to get up and "oil the shields!"

Anointing with oil can mean a lot of things, but in this season, I was praying and setting Doug apart for the spiritual battle I realized we were in. We needed God's power everywhere we walked. And though I didn't know it, Doug was walking in the back of the furniture store every morning, falling to his knees, crying out to God in prayer for deliverance.

When I took responsibility for my part and stopped blaming Doug (or anyone else) from stealing the life that I was supposed to live, things began to change. When I showed up to do my part, God showed up to do His. And wouldn't you know it, Doug and I grew closer together. God didn't wave a magic wand and *poof*, everything was better. It was slow and painful—but wholeness was beginning to be restored. This is when the next shifting season began—one I had been waiting for my entire life.

SHIFT #3: WIFEHOOD TO MOTHERHOOD

More than anything I wanted to be a mother, and I was willing to do whatever it took. Doug could see my intense desire for motherhood, as he finally said yes to having a baby. I was overjoyed to grow our family and become a mom. Doug and I immediately fell in love with our first daughter, Amaya Rose, and bought our first house. Our little family finally had a home. And I had what I'd always wanted: full-time motherhood.

I was surprised to find that even after Amaya came, the hollowness didn't disappear. I loved her with everything in me, but I still lacked the purpose I thought would appear. The healthy eating habits I'd built evaporated during my pregnancy, and certainly didn't come back on their own. Doug and I were still massively addicted to food. We were caught on the never-ending up-and-down of yo-yo dieting.

Every day I found myself on the couch vegging out to *Oprah*, a TV remote in one hand, a plump muffin in the other, and a toddler running crazy through the house. Again, not what I'd imagined my *Better Homes and Gardens* motherhood to look like.

I NEEDED MORE THAN SURVIVAL;

I NEEDED TO THRIVE.

It was time to pluck the weeds out of the garden of our lives. The things that were stealing the health from our bodies, minds, spirits, and marriage. As a mom, I realized this move was as much for Amaya as for Doug and me. Our family choices and habits would become hers. We started by saying no to the bachelor and bachelorette parties. We stopped hanging out with those friends all together. Instead of parties, I signed up for every mom's group I could find!

I was looking for a healthy community and a path to reclaim God's purpose for my life. I found my fellow bees and a fresh beehive to grow in.

I found mentorship, support, and challenge to become better. This shift in community made a massive difference. This was simply an expansion of a "me" to "we" mindset. I needed more than my own strength to become who God had made me to be. As I opened up, authentically sharing my story, I came to the realization that my parents had done the best they could with what they knew. But I still had unresolved trauma to work through. Parenting and self-help books led the way for my shifting season. I stopped blaming my bloodline and took responsibility to change it.

Personal responsibility became my mantra in motherhood,

marriage, and every in-between. Both Doug and I were hot in pursuit of becoming better together. We attended breakthrough marriage conferences (okay, sometimes I dragged Doug to them!), pursued mentorship, and pressed in with a small group of fellow contenders.

Through my time in the retail space, I had built up contacts, and I had influence in getting product placements in stores. So, I started my first side hustle in product placement. I started to earn money while being present for our growing family. During this time we had Katelyn, and Doug kept grinding at the furniture store. It felt like the clouds were parting and we were finally making some headway.

I thought I was helping to alleviate stress from Doug about our income, but I had no clue how deep our debt was actually growing. Doug tried to shield me from the anxiety and burden—but it had ballooned into $250,000 of business and personal debt. Some things were better, but others were far worse than I knew.

THAT'S THE THING ABOUT SHIFTS: JUST BECAUSE YOU'RE BREAKING THROUGH IN ONE AREA DOESN'T MEAN EVERYTHING ELSE SNAPS INTO PERFECTION.

However, it can be an anchor of change if you keep contending. I never gave up, and even though he wanted to at times, neither did Doug.

SHIFT #4: ENTREPRENEURSHIP

There's an old analogy about juggling our priorities in life. Some balls are rubber, and if you drop those, you can dust them off in time and throw them back into rotation. But some balls are made of crystal, and if you drop them, they shatter. I began to see our children as little crystal globes that I couldn't let down. Doug and I both knew we were playing a game with much higher stakes as our family grew.

Even though things were hard, Doug was an incredibly supportive father, and he worked hard to make me happy. I did my best to do the same for him, but we were both just trying to keep our heads above water. Our health was still out of control, and we had to come face to face with our unhealthy lifestyle on a fateful trip to Disneyland.

Disneyland was the be-all, end-all of family vacations to us. Doug and I were so proud and excited to give our kids an amazing time in the Magic Kingdom. The instant we entered the gates of Disneyland we were ready and raring to make a forever memory for our children, but we didn't make it far into the park before our bodies reminded us of the weight we had put on. Pretty soon our feet were sore from walking, our backs ached from carrying the girls, and our clothes clung uncomfortably - in all the wrong places - from sweat. What we intended to be a magical getaway for our family turned into us staring down the stark reality that we weren't the best versions of ourselves for our kids.

Not being able to keep up with our kids at Disneyland absolutely killed me. That was when Doug happened to see a friend on social media who had melted away their fat with probably the only program we'd never tried. I was sick and tired of failing at all the fad diets we had tried over the years, and I didn't have the will to try and fail again. I was barely hanging on with a one- and three-year-old at home, and even though I wanted change, this just felt like one more crystal globe I was going to drop.

Doug kept nudging me to kick my fear of failure. And let me tell you, this man has always been very persuasive and persistent! Finally, just like he gave in on making me a momma, I gave in on getting healthy with him. And I could hardly believe it, but this worked. Like *really* worked.

This shift into health became the anchor for our entire transformation. It was the breakthrough that led the charge to victory in every area of our lives. One at a time, the giants began to fall, and our inner Davids rose up (more on this in chapter 14). Food had become such a vice for us that I thought we'd never escape. But a week into our health journey I was down eight pounds. Within a month, I was down twenty. My habits were starting to change, and so was my relationship with food, myself, my daughters, and my husband. It was working!

I realized that if this worked for us, it could work for literally anyone. I saw a new opportunity for entrepreneurship, and with my newfound energy, I jumped on it. It was time to pay the gift of health forward and coach others to transformation. Deep down, this shift was pivotal because I also knew that I wanted to be known as something more than a mom or wife. As much as I still cherish both of those roles, I had value beyond them.

My victory over food became a launchpad for success. I became a part of a mompreneurs group, and I found that physical health was a *huge* problem for many other women in my community. For the first time I wasn't commiserating about weight gain over coffee and donuts; I was the voice of hope. Just by helping out a few friends, I was able to build something incredible. Our lives were finally changing.

I knew this for a fact when one day, Doug came back from the mailbox with his jaw on the floor. He held up a check from my business and asked, "Where did these come from?!"

"From coaching!" Not gonna lie, that moment felt amazing.

My pain point had become my purpose point, and Doug began to see the unbelievable blessings coaching others afforded to us. We started working together again, and we realized we worked incredibly well together now. Before, we had lacked the structure to bring our complimentary abilities to life. We were selling furniture then—but now, we were serving people. In this new transformation business, we found what we had been created to do. Coaching was the culmination of the preparation and pain that we had gone through.

Where our first business put us at odds, coaching brought us together. Every shift, from marriage, to personal responsibility, to motherhood, to entrepreneurship, required me to lay down my conception of what my life was going to look like.

I SURRENDERED TO THE PROCESS.

AND THAT ACT OF SURRENDERING OPENED

THE DOOR FOR MIRACLES TO TAKE PLACE

FIRST IN US, THEN IN OTHERS.

MAKE YOUR SHIFT

Shifts are hard. They are uncomfortable. They require the humility to admit what we've been doing isn't working anymore. They mean kicking real fear in the face and doing it afraid. They mean trusting that God's plan is actually better than yours, even if you can't see what's around the next bend.

One of Doug's and my favorite hikes is Camelback Mountain, rising from the desert valley floor. The summit towers over Phoenix and its suburbs, and you can see for miles. No exaggeration, we've probably taken thousands of people on this hike since moving to Scottsdale. What's interesting about this mountain is that the trail constantly makes you think you're about to reach the top. You think the summit is just around the next red boulder or rockslide you're climbing hand over hand. But you arrive, only to see more mountain ahead of you.

This journey is a great teacher. Every shift is like a curve in the trail. Right when you think you've arrived, a new challenge presents itself. But saying yes to the hard work is where the magic of transformation is at. My life looks a lot like that mountain—and I'm certainly not on the summit yet. However, with each curve, each decision to keep contending, each choice to kick fear in the face, the view gets more beautiful.

Success leaves clues. And the people I look up to are the ones who don't stop. Shift happens. Keep climbing.

I'll see you at the summit!

CAMELBACK MOUNTAIN, PHOENIX AZ

Revelations 5:5

"Then one of the elders said to me, 'Do not weep!
See, the Lion of the tribe of Judah, the Root of
David, has triumphed. He is able to open the scroll
and its seven seals.'"

CHAPTER 11

VICTOR'S
CROWN

If you go deep on any chapter, make it this one.

I have wrestled, prayed over, and gone back and forth with my editor about how to share the transformational power of worship with you. If there's any secret to my ability to contend and keep charging forward even when I'm afraid, it's this. Specifically, a song that's become an anthem for the ages.

It might resonate with you. It might not. But its words have helped me go to war for my family and future generations. It constantly reminds me that we don't fight alone; heaven itself is fighting for us. You see, my friend, I believe that eternal victory is already ours. When you awaken to this, it changes everything. And I seriously mean everything.

It changes:

1. How you show up in your marriage, even when pornography wants to rear its ugly head, shocking you like a thief in the night.
2. How you love and care deeply for those closest to you battling drug and alcohol dependency.
3. How you keep contending, even when it seems you've lost it all.

It doesn't matter what's going on because we are promised victory. Just like a gold medalist at the Olympics, we have the medal of golden victory hung around our necks. Or as it would have been in ancient times, the victor's crown is set upon our heads. Why? Because it was finished when Jesus paid the price at the cross two thousand years ago.

Jesus declared an end to the reign of sin and death over the lives of humanity and provided a way for us to walk in brand-new life. In victorious life! He became the once-and-for-all sacrifice paying for our evil, giving us His good in exchange. And with His goodness, grace, and mercy comes a crown of everlasting victory.

My friends, when we reconnect with this truth, it changes the very atmosphere around us. Clinging to this, meditating on this, and living in this victory has rewired my mind. I know, despite the heartaches and disappointments, I was put into my family bloodline for a reason. And so were you! There is a reason you're where you are and who you are.

No matter how weak or insecure you may feel right now, Jesus is always fighting for you. Like a force field or armor-bearer deflecting fiery arrows, Jesus shields and defends us. King David wrote about this in Psalm 3:3, saying, "But you, Lord, are a shield around me, my glory, the One who lifts my head high."

What's amazing is that he didn't write these words when things were good. He wrote this when his life was crumbling around him. His family was a shipwreck with his most important relationships having been smashed to pieces.

David's third son, Absolom, had murdered his brother and staged a coup, stealing the kingdom itself after declaring himself king. Everything David loved—his children and his country—were violently ripped away from him.*

SCAN ME

* YOU CAN READ THE WHOLE SAGA IN 2 SAMUEL 13-19.

Can you imagine the tragedy? The betrayal? The desperate heartache? But David knew, regardless of his chaotic circumstances, he served a God who was his defender, completely in control. And even more, He was the kind of God who reaches down in our sorrow, gently lifting up our chins to hold our heads high.

When I blasted this song in my car, I held on to God as my defender and felt as if angel armies thousands strong invaded my surroundings. Even when my most important relationships were strained, or Doug looked at porn again, or the people I cared about checked into a treatment center, I could find joy in God's presence through worship. Because I know God sees the victorious future even though I feel defeated now. Even though my present circumstances feel bigger than I can handle, he's already won.

From a young girl with a mom given a stamp of disease by the world to a teenager who didn't know how to connect with her father, His grace has met me in every season. Especially through this song, "Victor's Crown."

In this chapter, I want to share this powerful battle cry with you. No matter what is happening in your life and how high the forces against you tower, I believe strength and victory are available to you. Even if you don't feel strong right now, God does. Even if you don't have the faith to take another step, the Holy Spirit will move you. Even if you can't see a way out, Jesus is already on the other side waiting for you, wearing a victor's crown.

And for me, "Victor's Crown" continues to be my anthem whenever curveballs come my way. I blast this in my car, my house, my earphones . . . Wherever I am, I raise my hands and my voice, declaring these words as unshakeable truth.

Listen to the song and let the lyrics saturate your soul.

SCAN ME

· LISTEN TO THE SONG VICTOR'S CROWN HERE

PICK UP YOUR TORCH!

There's a book in the Bible called Lamentations. It's a collection of five poems reflecting on the massive tragedies God's people went through when the Babylonian empire took over Israel. It is not a happy book. But there is a tiny sentence that stands out to me. Lamentations 3:41 says, "Let us lift up our hearts and our hands to God in heaven."

A whole nation of people was dealing with the worst things that

Victor's Crown

You are always fighting for us, Heaven's angels all around

My delight is found in knowing, That You wear the Victor's crown

You're my help and my defender, You're my Saviour and my friend

By Your grace I live and breathe to worship You

At the mention of Your greatness, In Your Name I will bow down

In Your presence fear is silent, For You wear the Victor's crown

Let Your glory fill this temple, Let Your power overflow

By Your grace I live and breathe to worship You

Hallelujah

You have overcome, you have overcome

Hallelujah, Jesus You have overcome the world

You are ever interceding, As the lost become the found

You can never be defeated, For You wear the Victor's crown

You are Jesus the Messiah, You're the Hope of all the world

By Your grace I live and breathe to worship You

Every high thing must come down, Every stronghold shall be broken

You wear the Victor's crown, You overcome, You overcome

At the cross the work was finished, You were buried in the ground

But the grave could not contain You, For You wear the Victor's crown can possibly happen. The death of their families, the loss of their homes, and the erasure of their entire culture! But still, they're told to lift their *hearts* and *hands* to God. They're told to worship and cry out to God—specifically by raising their hands.

Why on earth would raising their hands matter? There's an amazing study that I think holds the answer. Social psychologist Amy Cuddy gave an amazing TED Talk where she unpacked the mysteries of what our body language says about us.*

SCAN ME

*****WATCH THE AMY CUDDY TED TALK *YOUR BODY LANGUAGE MAY SHAPE WHO YOU ARE***

Imagine a sprinter crossing the finish line ahead of the others. What would they do? Raise their hands in victory! It turns out that even people born blind, who've never seen anyone else raise their hands in that V shape, will do the exact same thing when they experience pride at winning. Lifting our hands is a hard-wired posture of victory. Isn't that amazing?

This is also one of the reasons we raise our hands when we worship. In my darkest seasons I've learned to worship my way out.

WORSHIP IS A WEAPON!

It is picking up the torch of hope and staying focused on the true north of His power in every situation.

I'm reminded of David dancing in worship with wild abandon, in 2 Samuel 6. He had just led thirty thousand young men into Jerusalem, bringing God's presence and the Ark of the Covenant with them. David leapt and sang and danced—but to Saul's daughter Michal, he had embarrassed himself. She said in verse 20, "How the king of Israel has distinguished himself today, going around half-naked in full view of the slave girls of his servants as any vulgar fellow would!" But

David replied in verse 22, "I will become even more undignified than this, and I will be humiliated in my own eyes. But by these slave girls you spoke of, I will be held in honor."

David was all about worshiping God with his full self, in total surrender. He was focused on God's presence and power. And this was for good reason. After all, his life was in constant danger from Michal's own father, Saul!

The lesson here is this. David didn't care about what he looked like or let anyone's opinions stop him from doing what he was gonna do: worship! This is power, my friends. This is fear kicking at its finest. Because David found constant strength, comfort, and vision in the worst of times in his Creator, not his critics! As we say,

OTHER PEOPLE'S OPINIONS
DON'T PAY THE BILLS.

When it felt like our family was crumbling from divorce and the loss of Christmases and holidays together, we worshiped through it. Some days it was the only way I could make it through the trauma and pain. Separation and betrayal threatened to become our story, but worship was a force that redirected my vision. There was an enemy coming after us with headshot after headshot; but in worship, you operate from victory, not defeat.

Worship has become as important to me as breathing. When it does for you, you're going to be blown away. Every morning, we blast worship at our house. Not just because we like the music (we do), but because we rely on its power. It shifts the atmosphere, regardless of what's happening in life.

FIND YOUR ANTHEM

Worship is partnering with heaven. That's what's happening in God's throne room right now, y'all! Check out Revelation 4:9–11:

"Whenever the living creatures give glory, honor and thanks to him who sits on the throne and who lives for ever and ever, the twenty-four elders fall down before him who sits on the throne and worship him who lives for ever and ever. They lay their crowns before the throne and say: 'You are worthy, our Lord and God, to receive glory and honor and power, for you created all things, and by your will they were created and have their being.'"

The mighty hand of God meets us here as we echo heaven. Worship brings the "super" into the "natural." I would create an atmosphere of worship because I knew it would flip a switch. It would hit me with energy—and it did every time.* God changes our story through worship, turning our pain into purpose. It's a guarantee that God can take our deepest pain and turn it into the greatest place to help people.

SCAN ME

* IF YOU'RE NEW TO WORSHIP MUSIC, YOU CAN LISTEN TO THE FEAR KICKER'S ATMOSPHERE OF WORSHIP PLAYLIST ON SPOTIFY

FRIENDS DON'T LET FRIENDS WORSHIP ALONE

In 2017 and 2018 Doug and I were drifting. We had tried numerous churches, but they just didn't click. We'd started giving up a little bit. But I'll never forget a conversation with Pastor Marcus Jones, a close friend, business partner, and amazing voice of godliness in our life. I explained our situation, that we couldn't find a safe place to land, given the type of people we are.

He simply said, "Thea, there is a church out there for you. You've gotta keep knocking."

DOUG & MYSELF WITH JEN & MARCUS JONES

It was such a simple encouragement. But God strategically placed him in our lives in this season. We were in deep pain and frustration, but here was Marcus acting as a guardrail, keeping us from flying off a cliff. He encouraged me to never worship alone. We weren't simply made to worship; we were made to worship *together*.

Thank God we didn't give up. That was when we found One Church Scottsdale*, a major breath of fresh, life-giving, Jesus-worshiping air we'd been missing in the desert valley.

SCAN ME

* CONNECT WITH ONE CHURCH SCOTTSDALE ON FACEBOOK HERE

I remember the very first Sunday we visited, we belted out a hopeful, happy song declaring Jesus's victory. And it washed over us like a promise from God Himself to never leave us or forsake us. There was freedom. But it wasn't the kind of freedom I could find alone in my prayer time. It was the kind of freedom that is shared, communal. I was reminded that we couldn't do this life on our own.

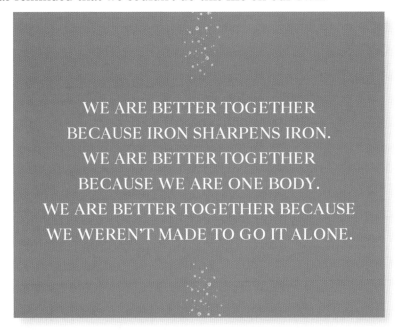

WE ARE BETTER TOGETHER
BECAUSE IRON SHARPENS IRON.
WE ARE BETTER TOGETHER
BECAUSE WE ARE ONE BODY.
WE ARE BETTER TOGETHER BECAUSE
WE WEREN'T MADE TO GO IT ALONE.

Don't give up hope that there's a community for you. There are people who are headed to the same place you are, cut from the same cloth, ready to contend at your side. God has them on standby waiting to edify you, speak life and encouragement over you, and keep you accountable.

Marcus's words that there was a church for me were a life saver. There is a community for you too. Maybe you just haven't found it yet. There is hope for you on the other side of what you're going through. There is a new story being written. And there's a community praying for you already!

We're all worshipers. You are a worshiper. The question is, what are you worshiping? You're designed to shift the atmosphere. Worship does this. You're made to see heaven's throne room invade your home. Worship invites this. You're made for victory. Worship fights for this.

The victory is yours, so grab hold of it. And it's been through the posture of worship where I've seen the pain obliterated. The end of the story is not loss. Jesus didn't just come to die—He came to rise up and give abundant life (John 10:10).

Find your anthem, like I found mine in "Victor's Crown." Shift the atmosphere in your home with worship, wielding it as a weapon in the darkest valleys. Most of all, unite with God's people, raising your hands and lifting your voices together. Don't give up, Fear Kicker. Worship.

You don't have to do this alone. And not only do you have people to link arms with, you have God Himself, your defender and shield. If this is brand-new and you want access to this power, you can have it right now. Simply surrender your life to the Savior of the World, Jesus Christ. The one who loves you and has been chasing you since you were born. He wants to be your helper, defender, savior, and friend.

Jesus, I put my faith in you, believing that you died for my sin and rose again from the grave. I believe you have won and I get to live from that place of victory. Thank you for salvation, new life, and your Holy Spirit. Now I live and breathe to worship you.

Whether you just prayed along with me for the first time or are choosing to recommit your life, let me know. I'm on this journey with you.*

SCAN ME

* CONNECT WITH ME HERE

Isaiah 43:15-16

"I am the Lord, your Holy One, Israel's Creator, your King.' This is what the Lord says - he who made a way through the sea, a path through the mighty waters..."

CHAPTER 12

I LOVE JESUS
(BUT I CUSS A LITTLE)

It was 1 a.m. on a ship in the Mediterranean Sea, and I couldn't sleep.

Earlier that day we'd sailed by the colorful houses of Cinque Terre. The iconic homes almost stack up on each other, perched on a cliff's edge overlooking the ocean. We'd seen the Leaning Tower of Pisa and taken the fun, touristy photos with our kids. But now, when I should have been sleeping, getting ready for our next day's adventure in Rome, I was beside myself with heartache.

As a busy mom and business owner, I'm not typically a news person. I'm usually out of the loop on a lot of things. But whenever something notable happens that Doug thinks I'll need or want to know, he tells me. That day was one of those times. I was reeling from sadness, and even anger, that welled up inside of me.

So I got up out of bed, threw on a black hoodie and my glasses, and made my way to the top balcony of our cruise ship. No one was around. I pulled out my phone, pressed record, and started to process the news I'd heard just a few hours before.

WHO ARE YOU?

I remember my girls had asked me, "Mommy, when you were little, what did you want to do when you grew up?"

The faces of my aunts Moni, Mici, JoDi, and Kathy flashed through my mind. I saw my Uncle Marty, my Grandma Edith, and Grandma Frey. My cousins Dawn and Laura popped into my head too, alongside so many others. From a very young age, they showed me Jesus's true, authentic love. Because of them, my soul caught on fire for Jesus. So, I explained to my girls that all I had wanted to do was share that fire, hope, and love with the world.

But over the course of this thing called life, hard things had happened. As a small-town Iowa girl, there were many things I never thought I'd have to journey through. There were so many moments where I thought, *This isn't how it was supposed to be!* I felt loss, pain, and confusion.

Really, what my girls were asking was, "Mommy, who are you, and is that who you'd always wanted to be?"

This question was especially poignant because that night, I'd learned that two people who I had admired for many years had taken their own lives. Suicide happens every day, but it was all over the news because within a week, two inspiring people had taken their lives: Kate Spade and Anthony Bourdain.

Kate was a fashion icon and pioneer. She had built a massive brand loved by millions, myself included—and that work had inspired me to create a brand of my own, Kick Fear in the Face! The mission of Kick Fear is on every page of this book, but the apparel line was, and is, all about encouraging people to rise up against the number one killer of dreams: fear. Kate created an empire in an extremely competitive marketplace, a remarkable thing to do.

At the time, she left behind her husband and a thirteen-year-old daughter. They were heartbroken. But her husband explained that she had been battling fierce anxiety and depression. Her family's pain broke my heart—but so did her pain. Because *I had felt that*. I had just pulled through a season where the whispers of suicide called to me in the night. Where pain nagged at me and wouldn't go away. I saw part of myself in Kate, and it wrecked me.

GET THE F*** AWAY!

If you've made it this far, you know that I believe in you. I know we each have a purpose on this planet. And that purpose is to break chains for ourselves so we can bring freedom to others. We also have a relentless enemy that stops at nothing to stop us dead in our tracks. I know this firsthand.

In October 2017, things were amazing. Our little Phoenix was healthy, our business was flourishing, we were plugged into a thriving beehive community, and we had incredible support and mentorship. Still, even with everything in its place, something was deeply wrong in my spirit.

As crazy as it sounds, a spirit of death was trying to take me out. By this, I mean a literal demonic attack in the spiritual realm. In our modern culture, it's easy to look past the invisible forces at work in the world. But they are real, active, and fiercely opposed to our lights shining bright with purpose.

I was truly in an all-out battle against the adversary of God's call on my life. If you've ever dealt with suicidal thoughts, we probably get each other. Even though I had such an amazing support system, the best husband and family imaginable, and a strong prayer life, this spirit still came after me hard . . . and nearly won. This is why the news about Kate Spade and Anthony Bourdain felt so personal—because I had been suffering the same feelings and thoughts.

Things might look great on the outside, but everyone is fighting a battle on the inside you can't see. Pain is present for people regardless of their bank account balance, social life, or beautiful family. Personally, I'm a dreamer and futuristic person. I want to change the world! So who better to take out?

If you want to change the world or even your little corner of it, you may have experienced these battles too. I think about Kate and Anthony, who brought joy and creativity into the world. Kate created experiences and shops that made you feel like a million bucks. She designed her lines with a price point for anyone. I had never wanted to have a Louis Vuitton or Chanel. I'd always wanted a Kate Spade. And before this trip, I'd finally bought one. It was devastating to hear this amazing woman took her own life.

Anthony traveled the world, shining light on incredible cultures and food. Watching and listening to him made you feel like you were walking ancient streets in Europe, finding the best cuisine off the beaten path.

These two very bright lights went dim—and I had been sliding down that path. So, this is a callout.

YOU'RE NOT ALONE. YOU'RE LOVED.

If you need to hear this, know that I have struggled with depression and the shadow of suicide too. But there is HOPE and LIFE on the other side of this battle.

I shared and processed these same thoughts in the video I recorded on the top level of our cruise ship. And in a totally raw, authentic moment, I said what I really wanted to say. And I'll say it again now.

Contending against deep depression and suicidal thoughts, I told Satan, *"GET THE FUCK AWAY in the name of Jesus!"*

That word might offend you—but it is the best way I can describe the intensity and energy I feel around this.

You met the high school Thea, the one who never cussed or stepped out of line. As a cheerleader, I was surrounded by coarse language on the football and basketball buses. I hated that kind of energy; it made me want to throw up. And I prayed for them. Early on in our marriage working in retail, I still didn't cuss. Those words were unnatural and just didn't ever want to come out of my mouth.

But then this thing called life hits you in the stomach. It knocks the wind out of you.

You go through pornography addiction in your marriage. *Smack.*
Divorce threatens your most cherished relationship. *Thud.*
You walk the tightrope of borderline bankruptcy. *Slam.*
Your family almost loses their farm. *Whack.*

My little halo tilted on that ship, a barrier finally broke, and I screamed at the enemy, expressing the truest horror of what I felt. And I meant it then just like I mean it now. Not to offend, but to contend.

I was flooded with dozens of *THANK YOU!* messages after posting this video to social media.* So many people felt seen and heard, like they could find their own voice of resistance instead of suffering in silence. It brought me to tears that there were so many in my life fighting this battle in secret. I knew my rawness was the right call, even if it was uncomfortable for some—especially one person.

SCAN ME

* YOU CAN WATCH THE VIDEO POSTED TO SOCIAL MEDIA HERE

thank you

Yes!!! 🔥

i've felt this way too! thank you!

I needed that

love!

THIS!!

thank you! you said
what i've been thinking

thank you!

Glad I'm not alone

THE MESSAGE

Out of fifty thankful messages about that video for being unplugged and on fire, one showed up in my messenger inbox that drowned out all the positivity. Someone close to our family called me out for cursing. This person didn't say anything about my struggles or pain; they simply quoted some Bible verses at me and said:

> Thea, you just never do that. It's not the way you deal with things. You unleashed the Devil's power in your life by letting that word come out of your mouth.

Wow. This thing called life hit me when I was down, but the shots that stung the worst were thrown by the people I loved most. I was so angry because those words rang hypocritically. Even though they were like family, they certainly did not have the mentorship equity to speak so harshly to me—especially over text!

This destroyed me. I blocked this individual on social media and carried anger for five years. I was so upset that they would respond to my pain with petty judgment. I felt totally justified. But this relational trauma wouldn't go away. Every few months it resurfaced. So, every few months, I crammed it back down into the basement of my heart. Until one day, I couldn't ignore it any longer.

I called the person and had an authentic, and definitely difficult, conversation. In the end, it turned out that that one little word poked their own pain and shame. It turns out, they had used this very word in anger and hurt years before when they ended one of their most cherished relationships and stepped out of ministry. It's wild, but often people's negative reactions to our authenticity tell us more about them than they say about us. It wasn't about me. But as we cleared the air, a single question rocked me. They asked, "Thea, is there any way you can unblock me, so I can at least see pictures of the kids?"

Of course I did so and apologized for handling their criticism the way I did. They apologized too. However, I didn't apologize for being raw that night. There was seriously no other word in the English language that could describe my energy. The truth is, I love Jesus, but I cuss a little. And you know what? That's okay. Because our pain should be expressed, and God is a safe place for that.

Where else can you take the pain of suicidal thoughts?
Where can you bring your anger?
Where do you go when your most important relationships are broken?

You go to Jesus who doesn't want someone fake; He wants the real you. And while a relationship with Him isn't like waving a magic wand to make your hurt disappear in ten seconds, He is the best one to help you fight those battles. Because that spirit of death trying to take us out isn't an enemy we can put a restraining order against, call the cops on, or even kick in the face! It's sneaky, invisible, and cunning.

But my friend, we can stand on this promise declared by the Lord from Isaiah 54:17. "No weapon forged against you will prevail, and you will refute every tongue that accuses you. This is the heritage of the servants of the LORD, and this is their vindication from me."

Our new family heritage isn't a curse; it's a blessing. A blessing of strength and unbreakable defense. Those weapons can't win. Those whispers of accusation can't stick. There is a path forward that's already been paved, and we have a guide who's always at our side.

YOU ARE NOT ALONE

I ended the video that night praying for everyone who would watch it. For every mind buried in anxiety. Every heart gripped by fear. Every life threatened by death itself. And I want to extend that prayer to you and for you as well. I love you. Even though we may never meet each other on this earth, know that if you've contended with these things, I see you. I feel you. I get you. And you are not alone.

God, we thank You that You are sovereign, with us, and beside us. I pray for my friends who are struggling with depression, sadness, and hopelessness. Let them feel Your hope right now. Give them that peace that surpasses all understanding in Jesus. Guard their hearts and minds. Relax their troubled brain in Jesus's name. Help them lead by their actions, focus on what You've made them to create, and strengthen their intentions to give life to a world that so desperately needs it—first and foremost, in their own hearts.

Anything that's stirring in them that is not of you, we take authority over it in the name of Jesus and proclaim Your truth to set them free. Invade their lives with Your power and goodness. We surrender our hearts . . . Living God, please raise them up on wings like eagles. Give them the strength to run this race and not grow weary. And Jesus, give them your complete joy right now.

Amen.

Fear Kicker, there are giants to slay in our lives. The spirit of fear, depression, and even suicide may be trying to take us out—I know they have tried in mine. But let me tell you, we have the weapons to stop them dead in their tracks. Let's see what we've got in our arsenal and learn to slay like an absolute world-changer named David.

2018 Wood Family World Travels:
We began in Iceland then flew to Barcelona, Spain where we boarded our 14-day Holland America Cruise that took us through Spain, France, Greece, Croatia, Monaco, Montenegro, and Italy. We then stayed in Venice, Italy before traveling through Germany, Switzerland, and Austria. We ended in Paris, France and visited Disneyland Paris.

1 Samuel 17:45

"David said to the Philistine, "You come against me with sword and spear and javelin, but I come against you in the name of the LORD Almighty, the God of the armies of Israel, whom you have defied.""

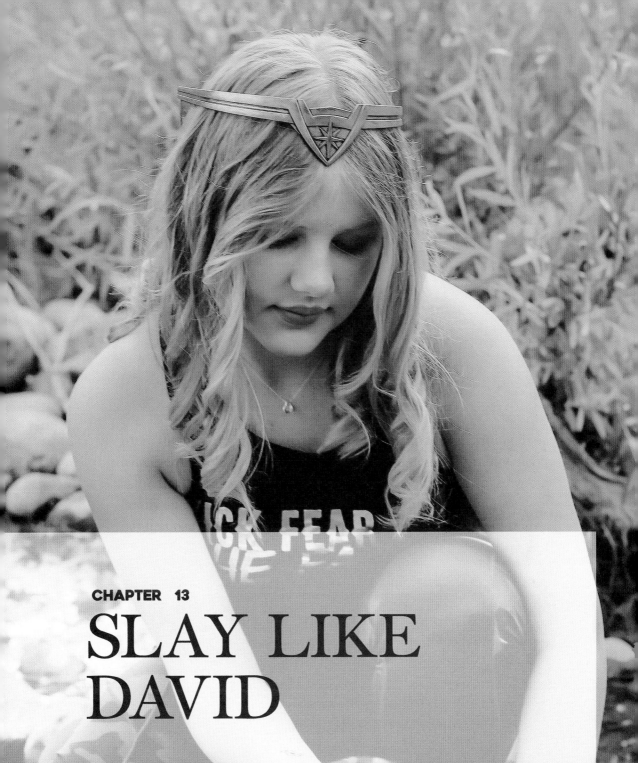

CHAPTER 13

SLAY LIKE DAVID

It's late on a Friday night and my mind is spinning. The soft glow of my computer screen flickers like a candle in my lap as I scroll through my news feed. My heart aches as I glance past another news story reporting that abortion rates are going up. My fingers brush the mouse pad and more painful stories scroll past, revealing deep hurt and growing darkness in our cities. Frustrated, I snap my laptop shut and beeline for a bottle of wine. As the bottle empties and my long-stemmed glass fills, I feel the weight of the week lift off my shoulders.

Ahh, that's better, I think, settling into the couch cushions. But was it really?

I had hit a season where this scene replayed itself more often than I would have liked. I carried a growing heaviness from thoughts of raising children in a world that seemed to get darker by the day. The worst tragedy was the destruction of thousands of unborn children every day. I wanted so desperately to contend for these silenced voices, but this giant felt undefeatable. These were forces simply too big for me to do anything about.

Dwelling on these tragedies day after day fueled a more personal giant in my life: alcohol. Using all my energy to fight off the depression left me exhausted. It was easier to pop a cork than to deal with the real stuff going on. But it wasn't like I had a problem, right?

I had unknowingly formed an emotional attachment. It was becoming my feel-good potion, settling in as part of my nightly routine. It helped me numb out and fall asleep, like a gentle medicine without immediate side effects. The problem was, this was how it had always started in my family. This giant had gained and held ground in my family bloodline for generations, starting after my great-grandfathers and uncles served in the world wars. And it was still there, biding its time for victory, standing unchallenged.

Whenever I had run to anything for comfort above God in my life, those things tended to become destructive vices. My sadness led me to take refuge in the wrong tower.

Overwhelming pain should be a trigger to run to our good Father.

He is our strong tower, the encircling wings of love, and a shield of protection.

Without this heavenly peace, I numbed out night after night. Some people may look at my life and see someone who has it all together, but I assure you that isn't the case—and wasn't especially at that time. I am working out my faith. He's not finished with me yet, and I had come to a spot where I was exhausted and nearly threw in the towel.

As we've journeyed together in this book, I've shared many hard seasons like this. There was always a way out, a path forward. Sometimes it was grit and hustle. Other times it was worship and prayer. And while those practices have been powerful throughout my life (and still are), I felt stuck when I tried to break out of this addictive cycle with alcohol. I wanted the numbness. I wanted the overwhelming feelings and pain to disappear. But I learned something so powerful in that season: we can't always rely on the same escape route in every situation, especially as we grow older.

God wants to deliver us, but He doesn't always do it in the same way. Few people's lives have taught me this as much as King David's in the Bible. Outside of Jesus, he's the most famous biblical king. Even if you didn't grow up in church, many of us know the story of David defeating Goliath.

IN THE VALLEY OF ELAH

David was the youngest brother of eight. He was the family sheepherder, spending sunny days and cold nights in the fields. To some of us, it sounds like a bit of a dull job. But as an Iowa farm girl, I can tell you that crazy things can happen in those fields—especially when there are predators hanging out, licking their lips while looking at your livestock.

In 1 Samuel 17 we listen in on David's conversation with a king named Saul (who he would eventually replace . . . more on that later). The Israelite army was lined up on one side of the Valley of Elah, and their enemies, the Philistines, were encamped on the other. Every day, a literal giant named Goliath marched out with his shield bearer and taunted Israel's army. And every day, Israel's finest warriors shook in their sandals.

Bible scholars think Goliath was probably around nine feet tall. He wore extreme armor that looked like metal fish scales, carried a spear that weighed thirty-three pounds, and wielded a fifteen-pound sword. Goliath's challenge was that he would face any Israelite in one-on-one combat, and whoever won the battle won the war for their country.

Goliath put everything on the line—and a young shepherd named David was ready to cross that line.

When David heard Goliath's wager and disrespectful rants, he was angry and had a conversation with King Saul. In 1 Samuel 17:34–36 he said, "Your servant has been keeping his father's sheep. When a lion or a bear came and carried off a sheep from the flock, I went after it, struck it and rescued the sheep from its mouth. When it turned on me, I seized it by its hair, struck it and killed it. Your servant has killed both the lion and the bear; this uncircumcised Philistine will be like one of them, because he has defied the armies of the living God."

Sure, he'd tended his dad's sheep. But the fields were places of battle. Before this giant, there were bears and lions.* And David didn't have the backup of an army or king's guard. He just had his courage, his hands, and his God. So he said in verse 37, "The Lord who rescued me from the paw of the lion and the paw of the bear will rescue me from the hand of this Philistine."

SCAN ME

* LEARN ABOUT A MODERN-DAY INCIDENT WHERE A MAN KILLED A MOUNTAIN LION WITH HIS BARE HANDS

You see, Goliath, and even David's own brothers, believed it was impossible for David to win. David knew it was impossible to lose.

King Saul bought in on David and sent him down into the valley to fight the giant. A creek bed lies at the bottom of the Valley of Elah to this day, filled with smooth white stones, tumbled and worn by the water. David scooped up five of those stones; and in a smooth, practiced, lightning quick motion, he slung just one straight into Goliath's skull. The giant was challenging, confident he'd crush this little "dog" (as he called David) in a fight. But David knew better and hit him right where Goliath was weakest: the forehead. Then as the Philistine army panicked and fled, David marched up to Goliath's body and cut off his head with his own sword.

I don't know about you, but this is how I want to handle my giants!

When alcohol invites me to numb out . . .

When pornography wants to weasel its way back into my husband's life . . .

When lies try to invade my children's minds . . .

I will choose the stone God has set between me and those giants and hurl it with all my strength. Because David taught a lesson for the ages:

EVERY GIANT HAS A WEAK SPOT

AND GOD WILL ALWAYS PROVIDE

A WAY TO TAKE IT DOWN.

FIND YOUR FIELD

What about you? What giants are trying to take you down? Where is your Valley of Elah, the place where the fight keeps going down? The place where every morning, afternoon, or late at night when you're alone, they prowl back and forth, taunting you, breathing lies, and trying to convince you that they've already won?

Let me encourage you to take a step back and find a new way to see this fight. The Israelite army was camped across from the Philistines, day after day. They had bought into the lies. Fear kept them silent. Inaction dominated every one of them. But David was different. Why? Sure, he was a man after God's own heart (1 Samuel 13:14); he was also an outsider. He came in from the fields where he worshiped, prayed, and experienced God's presence. David lived in a secret place where the rules were different. In the fields, you didn't hide from danger behind the person next to you. You couldn't wait for someone else to take action because you were the only one!

So, when David showed up to the Valley of Elah, he saw things differently. He saw the giant for what it was: a temporary enemy who was about to get its butt kicked. David kicked fear in the face in the valley because he'd made a lifestyle of it in the field.

He hadn't made peace or agreements with the culture of fear in the Israelite camp. He had a God perspective and total confidence because he served the God who always came through. The God who partners with the action takers, Fear Kickers, and giant slayers. David's confidence came from experience.

I believe God still partners with and prepares, us. Stage by stage, we fight lions, bears, and giants. Goliath doesn't look so big when he's standing next to the God of the Universe! Israel's warriors were waiting for someone else to lead. But when David stepped up, he didn't even need all five stones that God had prepared. He only needed one.

Are you living in the field or the fearful camp? God prepares His warriors in the field; so when they contend with giants in the valley, victory isn't impossible, it's inevitable.

NEW SEASONS, NEW STRATEGIES

Fast forward around twenty years and David the Giant Slayer is king. He's won battle after battle, written dozens of psalms, and has the respect of both his kingdom *and* his enemies. In 2 Samuel 21, we find David at the forefront of a battle against giants much like Goliath. He's forty years old now, and I relate to him so much. As I write this, I turn forty next month. While David fought literal giants, I contend against spiritual giants every day—and so do you.

What's interesting at this stage of David's life is that what used to work was failing. In an amazing message called "Same Devils, New Levels" (that I encourage you to listen to!), Pastor Steven Furtick helped me catch some things I want to share with you.* David was fighting the Philistines for the millionth time. It says in 2 Samuel 21:15, "Once again there was a battle between the Philistines and Israel. David went down with his men to fight against the Philistines, and he became exhausted."

SCAN ME

* **SAME DEVILS, NEW LEVELS PODCAST BY PASTOR STEVEN FURTICK**

"Once again."

Have you ever felt like that? A giant returns and you think, "Oh, not this again! How can I still be fighting insecurity? Fear? Porn? Gossip? Gambling? Drugs?" I *feel* those words "once again." And that was David's life here. Only now, David's previous fighting strategy failed. He'd defeated Goliath by stepping out and leading the charge. But this time he almost got himself killed.

The battle plan was always the same: David charged down center field with his mighty men swinging swords on either side. This was their formula for success. David cut through hundreds of warriors like a hot knife through butter. He faced off against kings and brought them down with his sword. David kicked fear in the face for breakfast. David's strategy of charging head first at the enemy hadn't worked just a couple times, it had worked every time.

Except this time, he was *exhausted*.

I know this is when my giants come at me the hardest. When I'm weary, burned-out, running dry, and don't have much fight left in me. This is where David found himself on the battlefield.

When your season shifts, it's time to switch strategies. David was learning that what worked two decades ago wasn't going to work today. How many of us are still hammering away with the same strategy but the season has shifted?

If you feel like your giants have been kicking you in the face lately, consider this: has your season in life changed? Here's what this looked like for David. He was tapped out on the battlefield fighting a giant named Ishbi-Benob. David was in big trouble. This line of giants, called descendants of Rapha, stretched back for generations. David was given the chance, just like us, to be a chain-breaker against generational giants. In this moment, he was contending for every ancestor back to Noah and every descendant all the way to Jesus.

Everything was on the line and it seemed like the giant had David cornered. Then God's new strategy for giant slaying came bursting into view. In 2 Samuel 21:17 we read, "But Abishai son of Zeruiah came to David's rescue; he struck the Philistine down and killed him. Then David's men swore to him, saying, 'Never again will you go out with us to battle, so that the lamp of Israel will not be extinguished.'"

This is the power of community. Abishai saw his king in trouble and stood in the gap for an exhausted David. David had to shift the spotlight away from himself and lean into his community. There comes a time when every great leader needs to step back and let the community he has duplicated himself in become heroes in their own right.

David tried to copy and paste his old strategy in a new season and it almost cost him, and Israel, everything. My friends, future generations are counting on us to slay our generational giants. They desperately need us to show up and win—but our strategy will change as we grow. David couldn't sprint full speed ahead any longer. As Abishai said, the light of Israel was in danger of being extinguished. Abishai saw how much was riding on David, so he told him, "We're never going to do it that way again!"

I want to make the important distinction between weak and exhausted that Steven Furtick points out in his sermon. David was not a weak person. You are not a weak person. I am not a weak person. But if you would have walked in on me drinking wine night after night, you might've judged me a bit, thinking, "Whoa, Thea . . . You're getting a little out of control."

It's tempting to look at someone (or even yourself) in their most exhausted state and label them as weak. Instead, we need to see exhaustion as a check engine light flashing on our dashboard. It's saying, "Hey, lean in to your community here and tap into a new level of strength." There comes a time when we simply can't contend against our giants the same way we used to.

Our strategy must match our season.

This story ends with a massive lesson in humility. Imagine David, this mighty king of legend who has won every trophy of battle through God's power and the grit in his belly, coming to grips with this new season of delegation. Proverbs 27:6 tells us that wounds from a friend can be trusted, and I'll bet David's pride was wounded when he listened to Abishai telling him he couldn't do things that way any longer. Not an easy pill to swallow—especially for a king! However, David chose the path of wisdom and never went into battle again. Because of that choice, watch what happens.

- Verse 18, one of his men slays a giant.
- Verse 19, Goliath's brother is slain by a warrior in David's tribe.
- Verse 20, David's brother slays another descendant of Rapha.

Like dominos, giants fell in waves after David saw the season shifting and switched his strategy. Remember, chains break forward and backward. Freedom ripples through our bloodline and in our community.

FATHER OF A GIFT

How you respond to your Abishai will determine your outcome. David received his help and listened to his advice, and as a result his community mobilized to achieve way more than he could have on his own.

Are you pushing your Abishai away? Do you accept help when you're at the end of your strength? Will you receive the word of tough love from a friend? Abishai's name means "father of a gift." Maybe God has someone carrying His gift to you, but you're stuck in your old strategies. Release your pride and receive the gift of the Father.

What did I do in that season when the giant of alcohol lined up across the valley? Exactly what I'm doing now—I invited others into the fight with me. I pulled my beehive community close. This wasn't a fight God called me to win on my own. He'd already given me a group of Abishais ready to contend with me—and I was ready to contend for them too.

Where are you saying no to the Father's gift when you should be humbly receiving His divine support? No matter how isolated you think you are, there is always a way out. I had been stuck in a season of turning to a couple of glasses of wine in the evenings to battle depression instead of running to the Father. But I found my way out by opening up to the community around me. We are better together. It takes strength to let an Abishai in to help and to say the hard things we need to hear.

Some people keep their enemy close and their Abishai far away. Are you surrounding yourself with a supportive beehive of giant slayers, or are you cornered and alone? Are you spending five hours on Facebook scrolling and only spending five minutes in the presence of the Father of good gifts?

Bring your community close around you and watch your giants fall.

size of a mustard seed

CHAPTER 14

YOUR
SHIELD

I love superhero movies. Most of all, *Wonder Woman*. If you're unfamiliar, let me introduce you. Her real name is Diana, a princess from an exotic island nation called Themyscira. She's the daughter of Zeus and, spoiler alert, has superpowers like superhuman strength, speed, and flight. Add to those powers a magical lasso, indestructible bracers, and a shield made by Greek gods, and you've got quite the Fear Kicker! But out of all her armor, her shield is my favorite. And there is one scene from the 2017 movie that inspires me the most.

Diana and her combat crew are fighting Germans during World War I in the Belgium village of Veld. It's all old stone, gray streets, and collapsed buildings. Gunfire and grenades explode all around them as they scramble through alleyways, trying to stay alive. Diana takes down soldier after soldier, smashing them with her shield, bracers, or boots. But at the center of the village, they run into a problem: a sniper hidden in a high bell tower.

Three of her fellow good guys dash into the open courtyard below the bell tower, totally exposed to the sniper, and lug a huge riveted metal sheet onto their shoulders. One of her allies, Steve Trevor, then calls out from beneath the metal sheet, "Diana, shield!"

SCAN ME

YOU CAN WATCH THE AMAZING SCENE HERE

Y'all, this is my goose bumps moment!

Diana sprints toward the makeshift launching pad, leaps onto it, and then springboards dozens of feet into the air. She raises her shield and smashes into the bell tower, taking out the sniper. She turns defensive armor into a powerful weapon. Her shield defends and attacks. And it's an incredible metaphor for the armor we have access to today—and the action it empowers us to take.

CATAPULT YOUR LIFE
THROUGH ACTION

I love that moment in the movie so much because it reminds me of my relationship with God. There's a fight of good versus evil. Everything is on the line. Then I hear my name and am given a command:

"Thea, pray . . . !"

"Thea, serve . . . !"

"Thea, give . . . !"

"Thea, love . . . !"

"Thea, forgive . . . !"

We live in the middle of a world war raging in the spiritual realm. Every day there are bombs and bullets, fiery darts and grenades, schemes and tactics trying to take God's people down. But every day, we have the chance to align ourselves with God's rescue mission to liberate millions of people.

I believe our role is to listen to God and then take immediate action, just like Diana. No hesitation. No second-guessing. When God prompts you to do something, do it right away! Why? Because it could be the gateway for thousands upon thousands to find a breakthrough!

Get into immediate action. From daring leaps into enemy fire to small, obedient steps.

My friends, action diffuses fear. If you want to catapult your life past fears like the chains of people's opinions, it's time to get moving. Growing up, my parents were action takers. They didn't sit still much because there was always work that needed doing. Hay didn't bale itself! I learned to value action from a young

age. Work was a good thing, and we got our stuff done every day whether or not we felt like it. The ability to do what needs done, when it needs doing, regardless of how you feel, is a critical life skill. And I'm grateful I learned it.

What's interesting is that there's a word so many of us aspire to, but we treat it like a feeling rather than a choice. That word is "love." As a wife, a mother, and an entrepreneur, I've learned that "love" is the greatest action word of all time. To catapult your life into significance is gonna take work—and that work is love.

The most famous verse in the Bible is probably John 3:16. Even if you're not a church guy or gal, you've probably heard or seen it: "For God so loved the world that he gave his one and only Son, that whoever believes in him shall not perish but have eternal life." Now, read that verse again. Slowly. And really think about two words: "so loved."

Did you do it? Okay, what do you think "so loved" means? Usually we think they mean "so much"—as in a whole lot of love! Such intense love that God would send His own Son to die in our place and give us the gift of eternal life. Yes, it definitely means that. However, that stops short of its full meaning.

Another way "so loved" could be translated from the original language is "in this way." Let's reread the verse with this new phrase. "For God loved the world *in this way*, that he gave his one and only Son, that whoever believes in him shall not perish but have eternal life."

Do you catch the difference?

God's love is a verb. God doesn't simply experience a feeling or emotion of love toward us (though He does). His love is more than affection; it's all-out commitment. God loved the world by taking action, and Jesus kept that action going all the way to the cross, dying for our sins so we could have forgiveness, life, and eternal security.

The same author of the Gospel of John, where that famous verse comes from, wrote a few other letters. In the first letter, in 1 John

4:8, he said, "Whoever does not love does not know God, because God is love." Check it out. God is love, so we see real love in who He is. Love is a verb, so real love is action, not just emotion. God loved through action that cost Him everything so we could have eternal breakthrough.

We get to live abundantly because He *fully* loved. That's how God's family does it. Sometimes we don't feel like loving, but we do it anyway. Sometimes we're scared of loving someone because it seems hard, but we love afraid. We live with a mindset that says, "I'm going to love you today no matter what." Now, if love is the action that sends us hurtling into battle like Wonder Woman taking out that sniper, what kind of gear do we have for this fight?

OUR GEAR FOR THE FIGHT

Have you ever heard of the Full Armor of God? It's lingo that comes from a Bible passage in Ephesians 6. It was written by a great missionary named Paul who actually wrote about a fourth of the New Testament. He describes a great spiritual war that we live in every day. We are on the frontlines of an ancient fight that's been raging since the beginning of humanity. And the ultimate prize is every soul in every person who's ever lived.

Paul was a Jewish man who was also a Roman citizen. Every day, he saw hardened Roman soldiers decked out in their armor and loaded up with weapons. He took their gear and used it as an analogy to show us the armor of heaven available to us as we join God's rescue mission for humanity.

In Ephesians 6:11–12 he tells us, "Put on the full armor of God, so that you can take your stand against the devil's schemes. For our struggle is not against flesh and blood, but against the rulers, against the authorities, against the powers of this dark world and against the spiritual forces of evil in the heavenly realms."

We have access to indestructible armor like Diana's shield. It powers us to take our stand to contend against spiritual forces of evil. These forces are coming after our culture to spread lies and make fear go viral. They're attacking our minds, marriages, and most of all, our God-inspired families. What does this heavenly armor look like?

Paul says in verses 14–17, "Stand firm then, with the belt of truth buckled around your waist, with the breastplate of righteousness in place, and with your feet fitted with the readiness that comes from the gospel of peace. In addition to all this, take up the shield of faith, with which you can extinguish all the flaming arrows of the evil one. Take the helmet of salvation and the sword of the Spirit, which is the word of God."

Here's what we've got:

1. The Belt of Truth
2. The Breastplate of Righteousness
3. The Boots Ready to Share the Message of Jesus
4. The Shield of Faith
5. The Helmet of Salvation
6. The Sword of the Spirit

We can pray these on every day. Paul even asked his friends to pray for him so he could declare the message of Jesus *fearlessly*. That's right, Paul was a major Fear Kicker. This armor was one of his greatest strategic advantages.

In my life, I've experienced power from every piece. Holding on to truth holds everything together for me. I lean into God's promises, trusting in them instead of my feelings. I declare His power over every situation in my life—and even in this world. My core is protected by righteousness, and not my own because I'm so perfect and amazing, but Jesus's, because He was and is perfect and amazing. Fear Kicker, if you know Jesus and have the Spirit of God living inside of you, when Father God looks at you, He doesn't see a guilty person who should live in shame, blame, and fear. He sees Jesus's perfection and glory— He sees beauty instead of ashes and gorgeous robes instead of grave clothes (Isaiah 61:1–3)!

I've also got those fear kickin' boots ready to take massive action and share this message of hope, freedom, and breakthrough. Imagine what your life could look like if your default state was taking action, sprinting into the thick of the fight, instead of shrinking back.

That vision keeps me going because that's the kind of woman I want my kids to meet every day.

My salvation is the helmet that protects my head. God's Word is a sword nothing can stop. And together, these have catapulted me into action. But even Paul points out one piece of armor that's a little different than the others by saying, "In addition to all this, take up the shield of faith . . ."

It's almost like he's pointing out, "Hey, fellow warriors, make sure you don't forget this piece of equipment, because you're going to need it." And he then describes what it's capable of doing—"extinguish all the flaming arrows of the evil one."

Just like Diana's shield blocked every sniper bullet and fiery bomb, my faith shield has protected me through countless all-out attacks on my life, my marriage, my family, my health, my business, and even my relationship with God. So never leave home without that shield. Take it up. Charge enemy lines. And keep it raised high so it can catch and put out those flaming arrows our enemy never stops shooting at you.

LIVING ON THE FRONTLINES

We can pull heaven's armor into the now. At this very moment, you can gear up and go to work. We can hold the line of truth for future generations. We're in a war and we have a purpose. It isn't behind the frontlines.

Last chapter, we took a deep dive into David's life. Obviously, I love him, resonate with him, and learn so much about how to do life as one of God's people through his story. However, he was far from perfect. You might remember his famous scandal with a woman named Bathsheba. We read about it in 2 Samuel 11.

David's men were on the frontlines fighting a war. But instead of fighting alongside his men or providing strategic direction, King David was chilling at home, staying comfy in his palace. One day he was hanging out on his roof, wasting time, and then saw her . . . the beautiful Bathsheba. She was naked, taking a bath. Instead of looking away from this married woman and respecting her dignity and privacy, David watches. Instead of putting his strategic gifts to work for the good of his soldiers, he schemes how he can get this woman into his bed. In the end, David has her husband Uriah murdered to cover up his adultery after he sleeps with her.

Do you see what happens when we're not living on the frontlines? We lose focus. We forget about the fight. We ignore what's truly at stake! And I promise you, both from David's example and personal experience, nothing good comes from shrinking back and clinging to comfort, mindless pleasure, and distraction. It's easy to look at David's story from thousands of years ago and point fingers at him. But what does this same behavior look like today?

I doubt any of us are having soldiers murdered, but the same draw to comfort and chilling at the palace still has many of us in its grips. Let's call it out! It's time to stop binging The Bachelor and reading gossip magazines. It's time to quit sitting around like there's not an actual battle raging at our doorstep. It's time to stop playing beneath our purpose.

FRIENDS, WE ONLY NEED THE FAITH OF A MUSTARD SEED TO HAVE A SHIELD THAT CAN HANDLE EVERYTHING THE FRONTLINE BATTLE HAS TO THROW AT US.

And there are people who have lifted some heavy stuff for you to be where you are. They've fought hard and contended against those giants so you could have the freedom you've got now. It's time for you to jump, sprint, and charge full-on!

My parents were chain-breakers—and now it's my turn to keep making the way. World changers and Fear Kickers don't happen by accident. They're born of the choice to act, fight, and love. Maybe you've been stuck because of the sniper, that spiritual enemy who knows exactly what to fire your way. What fiery arrows have kept you pinned down and playing small? It's time to take them down.

I hear so loudly in my heart God's voice commanding, "Thea, shield!" Do you hear it? Do you feel it? Do you see where that enemy is, perched in a high place, keeping you stuck, making sure your boots are nailed to the ground (or your butt is glued to the couch)?

If you're here, let me encourage you. I'm raising my hand right now because I've been there too. If you've read this far you know that's true. So, I want to share with you how to start and get unstuck. Because we've talked about some pretty epic things. Big moments about wars and battles and fighting the forces of darkness. However, your fight doesn't have to start by organizing a million-person march in the streets. It might lead there, but I've found it can actually start in the simplest of places.

For me, living on the frontlines starts by getting up, putting on my makeup, my cute outfit, getting my workout in, and following my Spark Habits.

Big action is the product of many little actions.

Those daily action steps diffuse my limiting beliefs. I can always take action in these basic things. And you have the power within you to show up—after all, half the battle is showing up! I believe that the basic, seemingly mundane things we do today bash the enemy in the

face and are the beginning of our moment.

Getting ready is such a big deal because it energetically positions you to show up at your best. It's a statement to the world and yourself that you're ready to be serious. Ladies, there's something special about putting on your skinny jeans instead of staying in your yoga pants. Guys, maybe you need to shave today, swish some product in your hair, and dab on a little cologne.

I think of my gear like armor. That's why Doug and I designed our own clothes. Not primarily because we wanted to create another business, but because we wanted gear that expressed our purpose, passion, and impact. I found and made clothing that spoke to me and helped me partner with my future self instead of being partnered to my past. And what was that future? I was fitter. I sat at conferences with powerful people. I filled stadiums to inspire, share hope, and shine brightly. Being intentional with getting ready is about positioning yourself to accomplish your purpose for the day.

Another small but mighty action step is making your bed. There's a commencement address by Admiral William H. McRaven that you may have seen (and if you haven't, watch it now). After all his years of military experience, wartime strategy making, and leading thousands of soldiers, he said, "If you want to change the world, start off by making your bed."*

SCAN ME

* WATCH ADMIRAL WILLIAM H. MCRAVEN'S VIRAL COMMENCEMENT ADDRESS IF YOU DIDN'T WATCH IT WHEN I SHARED IT EARLIER IN THE BOOK—OR WATCH IT AGAIN

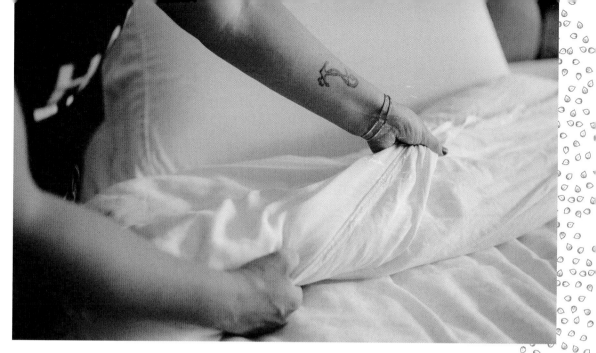

That's a pretty bold statement. But what he's saying is that winning the day is about starting with momentum. Your head hitting the pillow in victory tonight starts by how you begin your morning. Get dressed. Make your bed. Show up.

For me, working out is a major part of showing up. Years ago, I made an agreement in my mind that I didn't like working out. I told myself that I wasn't an exercise person and was convinced that it wasn't important for me. But when we agree with something, true or untrue, it means we go along with it as if it were true; and it shapes how we see ourselves and live our lives. I had to flip the tables and break with those agreements, thought processes, and the inaction they produced.

Here's the truth. Even if you feel like a poser and imposter, there are people depending on you to show up today. Did you know that? Someone needs to hear what God will lay on your heart. Someone needs to see you take that love action you didn't know anyone saw. And there are people in your beehive community holding that metal shield on their shoulders, straining under its weight, ready for you to show up and take the leap.

So gosh dang it, if that's who I want to become, why am I sitting around in my sweatpants?!

No matter where you're at right now, you can choose action, even if you're afraid. You can choose to rise up in the small ways so you can show up for the big battles. Are you going to wake up fifteen minutes earlier every day? Are you going to lay out your workout gear and running shoes the night before? Are you going to unplug the TV and hide your remote beneath that stack of books you should be devouring? Are you going to embrace structure to partner with your future self?

If I want to go impact communities like Diana, who saved a whole region, I've gotta show up every single day with my spiritual armor and physical armor on. Believe me, your faithfulness to impact the few will ripple out to transform the many. The domino effect will blow your freaking mind! But now it's time for you to pick up your shield and put on your daily armor.

These are the actions. This is how I show up in faith in the midst of divorce and addiction and hundreds of thousands of dollars in debt. This is how I get into action even when I'm shaking in my boots. This is how I stay focused even while trying to figure out how to parent a toddler and teenagers. This is how I keep my mind sharp and heart open in partnership with Doug, as a husband and business partner.

I am called to live on the frontlines. So are you. Now that we both have some inspiration and action steps to start with, we can look further ahead to find the surprising partner and mentor everyone has access to, but few will ever seek out.

It's time we partnered with our future selves.

SCAN ME

' KICK FEAR GEAR

Jeremiah 29:11

"For I know the plans I have for you," declares
the Lord, "plans to prosper you and not to harm
you, plans to give you hope and a future."

CHAPTER 15

PARTNERING WITH YOUR FUTURE SELF

One evening in 2012, Doug and I packed our coaching team into a conference room. Doug spoke first and shared part of our journey. At that time, he was working through a major identity shift. He used to be known as the furniture guy, but now he was a coach. People nodded along and scribbled notes as he shared, and I could tell people resonated with him.

As his talk came to a close, he asked everyone in the room, "What's the one thing holding you up?" The room was quiet as everyone's gears turned, thinking about that question. For most of us, we have a hundred things holding us up, right? If all we had was one big problem, we'd be in constant motion! But that isn't actually true. What Doug meant was, what's the root system beneath the surface that's keeping you from moving forward? The issue *beneath* the issue?

At that time we were coming out of massive debt of over $250,000, had just sold our house and moved, and were flexing our hustle muscles as we built our business. It was a lot of transition, but it also meant we were breaking through some serious junk. And because we worked with so many people, we were seeing patterns in what blocked people from moving forward.

Doug let the question hang in the air a bit longer as people thought, and then he turned to hand the mic to me. That was when I got a wild idea and asked Doug to keep holding the microphone for me. I had a key in my hand and gripped it tightly. Then I crouched and screamed, "Sometimes you just gotta kick fear in the face!" and then leapt off the stage in a flying kick!

I saw a sea of shocked faces as I flew toward the people in the front row. When I landed, I didn't stop. I ran up to one of the women and handed her the key. She had created incredible transformation in her life, radically growing in her health, mindset, and finances. I was proud of her and knew her transformation had inspired so many others even in that room. I also knew that when she started, she was afraid, but she did it anyway.

She took the key from my hand and had *no clue* what I was doing.

Then I told her to stand up and I asked the room, "How many of you are in this room because of her?"

Chairs shifted and the floor creaked as fifty people stood. She looked around, startled by the impact she'd had on so many people she didn't even know. Fifty people from different cities around the country had changed their lives, all because she said yes (and that was just a small sliver of the people she'd actually inspired). She kicked fear in the face and made the decision to take control of every aspect of her life. And her transformation inspired others to do the same thing. Then I pointed at the key she held.

"Every one of your hearts has a keyhole that was unlocked by this woman's actions. And guess what? Every one of you have keys to the hearts of thousands more. We can transform this nation and our world by kicking fear in the face together saying, 'I don't care what anyone thinks . . . I don't care who misunderstands me . . . I care about unlocking freedom for thousands of people!'"

I pulled this stunt because I had to honestly answer Doug's question as well. "What's the one thing holding you up?" The one thing that held me up for years was fear. It was the same thing that had kept so many in that room stuck. What I love, though, is that the one person who kicks fear in the face unleashes waves of breakthrough in their corner of the world—and even beyond.

The more Doug and I saw this scene play out, the less we lived according to our emotions. Doug lived with the mantra "make the daily commitment to be consistent," and I pushed myself every day to kick fear in the face. Even though this shift didn't make consistency or fear kickin' any easier, it always made it worth it.

This allowed us to see beyond these packed rooms and into filled auditoriums, where thousands of people would gather because we kept showing up. Kept loving. Kept serving. Kept working on ourselves to inspire our community. Our business and community grew like wildfire. Even though more faces were added every day, the heartbeat remained the same: help people get unstuck and fulfill their purpose.

THE SHORES OF GALILEE

Between then and now I've invested a lot into myself. I've worked to get in the room with the right people. And to be honest, I began to find myself achieving a level of success I never thought possible. However, even as I looked at the successes Doug and I had achieved, I was still dissatisfied. Somehow everything we'd built and done wasn't enough.

How is that possible? I thought. *I should be totally content. Isn't this enough?* But it wasn't. I'd found a new keyhole somewhere deep within my heart, but I didn't know where to find the key. Something was locked away and I desperately wanted to find out what it was.

Doug felt it too. So yet again, we invested thousands of dollars into a coach who could take us to the next level. We laid everything out on the table and shared our journey, where we wanted to go, and our inner dissatisfaction. What she said changed my life forever.

I thought she'd recommend a long-forgotten book, secret workshop, or exclusive conference that I'd never heard of. I expected some kind of ancient wisdom that had been lost to the ages. Instead, she showed me that the key to that locked door in my heart was in the last place I was looking for it: *in my own hand.*

She said, "Thea, we're going to partner with your future self. She will be your guide."

"What the heck?! Isn't your job to be my guide?" I replied.

She explained her role was to help me create space to form a new partnership with Future Thea. She invited me to go twenty-five years into the future and imagine the answers to a barrage of questions . . .

- What was that Thea doing?
- How was she acting?
- What had she accomplished?
- Who was she surrounded by?
- Where was she?
- How did the air smell?

Together, we painted a super vivid picture of what life looked like for her. All without limits.

This wasn't a question of what I could *reasonably* accomplish given my limitations, it was a question of what I would accomplish because I would slay every giant in my path. Going out twenty-five years was something I'd never even thought about. That was further than I'd ever imagined. I'd always thought about what the next five years might look like. But at this stage, we'd blown our five-year goals out of the water.

Suddenly the root system of my dissatisfaction was exposed. I didn't have a new vision for what we were building. We had everything we could ever want. Yet there I was, dissatisfied. Antsy. Feeling unfulfilled. So naturally, I ran to a coach screaming: "GIVE ME ANSWERS!" Notice this was an old strategy that had served me very well in many seasons. But with this new level, it was time for a new strategy if I wanted to slay like David!

Then that brilliant coach helped me find the only person who could give the answer I was looking for: future me. This wasn't an exercise that turned me away from God's direction either. Instead, it led me toward His face. Now, instead of asking God "Why isn't this enough?" I was really exploring "What are you trying to do through our lives?"

I closed my eyes, answered the questions, and here is the vision that unfolded before my mind's eye:

I felt warm sunlight on my face and smelled water. I could hear seagulls, the water lapping against the shore, and children laughing. Somehow I knew I was in Galilee. I could sense and feel it. I had been to an Airbnb in Galilee before—but that wasn't where I was. I was at my own home. My kids were chasing after my ten grandchildren who'd just arrived from somewhere else in the world. It was a holy moment in a holy place. And it was mine. The next morning, I saw myself waking up before sunrise, lacing up my shoes, and running in the morning air. I was so fit I nearly floated. Every stride felt right. I returned home from my route and Doug had opened the windows and doors to welcome the sunrise. It was getting hot, which meant one thing: we were going to hit the sea on our jet boat! We spent the day wakeboarding (yes, people do that behind jet boats!), swimming, playing, talking, and remembering.

That was the first time I met future Thea, and she took me out for a day on the Sea of Galilee with my family—and I gotta admit, I love that girl! Once I was there, it stunned me. I could genuinely see it, smell it, and hear it. A profound sense of certainty washed over me and I knew that was my life in 2045. I started partnering with Future Thea, bringing that future into the *now!*

The truth is that once you can see something behind your eyes, you can hold it in your hands. If you can imagine it, you can bring it into reality. Most of us simply don't take the time to sit with God and travel into the future.

Today, when I hear my future calling but the old Thea is stuck thinking small, I partner back up with my sixty-five-year-old self who says, "Thea, hey girl, how are you doing? Thank the old Thea who got out of bed today. But now let's get to work!"

As crazy as this sounds, Future Thea has become my greatest support and mentor (outside of God). I'm not looking for validation from people outside of her. I'm not waiting for permission from anyone else. This was a landmark moment because, for the first time, I wasn't striving for someone else's vision for my life. I completely released a need for anyone else's approval. And in that vision, that future on the shores of Galilee wasn't impossible; it was inevitable.

Now, when things get monotonous and consistent action gets hard, I have this thirty-thousand-foot view from God. I can zoom out and gain instant perspective on where my current circumstances fit within the bigger picture—and I can also feel the urgency of what's at stake. When I doubt whether or not I should really be pursuing these Galilee dreams, I remember that no one has set these standards for me. I set them for myself. Our future is driven by the mission and mandate God has placed on our lives. Because I promise you, that house on the Sea of Galilee represents millions of changed lives. It's just a little reflection of how God used the Wood Family to spark breakthrough in the nations!

PARTNERING WITH YOUR FUTURE SELF

My friend, I have two questions for you:
1. **What is the one thing holding you up?** What keeps you from daily actions toward those big dreams of yours? What keeps you pressing snooze instead of leaping out of bed with a fire in your heart? What keeps your mouth closed when you know you should be inviting people to partner with you?
2. **Twenty-five years from now, who is your future self?** What have they accomplished? What excites and motivates them? What are they thankful for that you did today that enabled them to be where they are?

Anytime I feel resistance, I have a little conversation with Future Thea. No joke, it feels like fresh strategy gets downloaded straight into my brain. I'm instantly filled with confidence to live unapologetically and own who I am, what I'm about, and where I'm going.

Like that wonderful coach Doug and I hired, I invite you to partner with your future self. Take some time to vividly meet them twenty-five years from now. I've found it helpful to write down what your future self looks like, acts like, has achieved, and believes.

Once you meet your future self (who you're going to love), here are some questions I use to reconnect with that vision when things are hard and I don't feel like showing up:*

1. What is my future self inviting me into?
2. What opportunities are being presented to me?
3. How am I growing in my confidence?
4. How am I embodying my future self today?
5. I can hear my future self calling but I'm <u>resisting</u> because . . .
6. I can hear my future self calling and I'm <u>embracing</u> this call because . . .
7. My future self is grateful for me today because . . .

Understand that this partnership, like anything worthwhile, is a process and takes practice. You're building a brand-new relationship with your future self. Relationships take time! I recommend doing this for thirty days in a row. This is the beginning of a divine relationship because you're meeting the person God is turning you into.

Along the way, you'll make some surprising discoveries about yourself. As I have continued this heart work, I saw the new face of fear trying to hold me up . . . not a fear of failure, but a fear of success. I feared the future because I had never seen a sustainable model of success. But it was time to break with the old narrative I was living in. I'd seen money flow through people's fingers like sand. I'd watched unwise choices break up marriages and destroy everything that had been built. But things shifted when I looked at the future God has for me rather than what happened to others.

SCAN ME

˙ I LEARNED THESE FROM THE BRILLIANT HELEN URWIN

We can't spend our lives looking in the rearview mirror. What does your future self see in you that you don't see in yourself? What will you do today that they will thank you for? Enter deeply into this process and find the key that's already in your hand!

OUR FAMILY VISITING THE SEA OF GALILEE

The dandelion

The dandelion is a symbol of hope, love, and happiness. The seeds are said to carry wishes for prosperity and new beginnings with them as they fly away into the sky.

CHAPTER 16

FIND YOUR
SECRET PLACE

Remember blowing dandelions as a kid?

When I was a little girl, a yard full of dandelions was a magical paradise. Over and over I'd pluck those fluffy white flowers and blow them everywhere. They danced with me in the breeze, soaring wherever they wanted. As a kid I didn't realize this, but a single dandelion seed can actually float for over fifty miles. (No wonder they end up everywhere!)

I remember feeling God's presence whenever I was outside picking dandelions, playing on my swing set, or running barefoot across our farm. I didn't watch much TV. Instead, my mom unleashed me to play outside whenever and wherever I wanted. And because I felt God with me, I talked with God.

Every day for hours I lived in a mystical land where I played and explored and learned to pray. I didn't realize I was praying; it was just a natural outflow of feeling close to Him. To my little mind, God's presence was always real and accessible. I felt it in the wind. I heard it in the rain. I touched it in the dandelions. And little did I know there was an even deeper lesson in those floating tufts of dandelion seeds.

In 2018, scientists from the University of Edinburgh made a discovery about dandelions.[*] They learned that the seed canopies create a vortex you won't find anywhere else in nature. When the wind blows from underneath the seed it flows out and around the fluffy white bits, then curls back on itself. This creates a tiny low-pressure air pocket just above the seed, allowing it to float unnaturally far.

SCAN ME

*LEARN MORE ABOUT THE FASCINATING DISCOVERY OF DANDELIONS HERE

I told you there was magic in those seeds!

This inspires me because now I see a secret that many have experienced, but few could explain. There is a secret spiritual garden for us. A special, sacred meeting place God creates to meet with us.

Wherever we are at in life, through Jesus, we have access to what the Psalms call the "secret place." And the secret place is a vortex that will carry us far and wide—much farther than we could ever fly on our own. I discovered this by accident as a little girl. But now, I return there every day and hold on to it with everything in me.

If you've done what I've encouraged you to do throughout this book, buckle up, because we're going to dive into the deepest, most wonderful aspect of the Fear Kicker's life: a spiritual, secret place where God desires to meet us and teach us.

HIDDEN IN THE ROCK

Jewish tradition has it that Moses wrote about this special place, saying, "He that dwelleth in the secret place of the most High shall abide under the shadow of the Almighty" (Psalm 91:1 KJV). Other translations call the secret place a shelter. Moses is talking about a place guarded by God Himself where we can meet Him. And Moses is someone who knew this place, and this God, well.

Moses was the man God used to lead His people out of slavery in Egypt. His story is filled with incredible miracles like the ten plagues of Egypt, the parting of the Red Sea, and even speaking with God like a friend. Check it out in Exodus 33:11: "The Lord would speak to Moses face to face, as one speaks to a friend. Then Moses would return to the camp, but his young aide Joshua son of Nun did not leave the tent."

Moses met with God in a secret place called the tent of meeting—fancy name, right? He also had an apprentice named Joshua (famous for stories like the Battle of Jericho in the Old Testament book named after him) who loved to spend time with God there too. He loved this secret place so much that he barely ever left it! Being in God's presence is powerful, profound, and transformative. You can't meet with God in the secret place and not leave just a little different than you came.

However, Moses's God story continues. His secret place wasn't simply a tent. There wasn't only one place to meet with God. Later in this same chapter we get to listen in on a conversation between Moses and God on a mountaintop. After asking God to send His presence with Israel wherever they went, he made an amazing request: "Then Moses said, 'Now show me your glory'" (Exodus 33:18).

God replied in verses 21–22, "There is a place near me where you may stand on a rock. When my glory passes by, I will put you in a cleft in the rock and cover you with my hand until I have passed by." God's glory, a burning, blinding, brilliant light, passed by Moses as he was tucked in a protected cleft in the rock. God made a secret place for Moses outside of the tent of meeting. Away from the Red Sea. Beyond the borders of Egypt. God met Moses, and He created an intimate place of connection with him, right where he was.

All Moses had was a hungry heart for God's glory and a mind set on obedience. This is still how God is today. He's not confined to a place or space. He wants to fill our hearts with His Spirit and meet us in a special place, just for us.

I was a three-year-old girl who felt God's presence. I still tap into that. For me, I love going into nature, high into the mountains, out on remote hikes, getting into the flow on a long run, or cruising on the water. This is where I meet God in my secret place. Yours will look different than mine. But it's not like you have to go to a magical tent or mystical mountain.

If you want a friendship with God, He'll meet you where you are at. He wants a relationship with us. God also told Moses that he knows him by name (Exodus 33:17). They weren't simply acquaintances. Moses didn't just know theology, doctrine, or stats about God. He knew Him personally. This is the purpose of the secret place.

From the beginning of time, God has had a plan for you. He put you in this moment and culture for a reason. Psalm 139 tells us that you are "fearfully and wonderfully made." You were created with a purpose. The secret place invites us into clarity and freedom—into

God's destiny for us. It helps us forget the opinions and expectations of others so we can flourish. It's a place outside of the work, hustle, and grind we can produce in our own power. It's about connecting with the ultimate power source and fountain of wisdom!

GOD, WHY DID YOU MAKE PEANUTS?

You might remember a man named George Washington Carver. He created hundreds of products from pecans, sweet potatoes, and of course, peanuts! However, the story of how he made his breakthrough with the humble peanut is my absolute favorite. Mark Batterson writes about it in his book *The Circle Maker*.

Carver worked for Booker T. Washington at the Tuskegee Institute. One day, Washington came to him with a problem. Carver had recommended that local farmers swap out their cotton crops for peanuts. By rotating the crops they would replenish their soil. However, there was a snag: peanuts weren't worth much more than the dirt they grew in. Nobody knew what to do with them. So suddenly, a bunch of farmers were about to have fields full of peanuts they couldn't make a dime from. This wasn't good.

However, Carver wasn't concerned. He simply replied, "All my life, I have risen regularly at four in the morning to go into the woods and talk with God. That's where He reveals His secrets to me. When everybody else is asleep, I hear God best and learn my plan . . . This morning I asked Him why He made the peanut."*

SCAN ME

* **READ ABOUT CARVER IN THE ARTICLE** *THAT SPECIAL PLACE* **HERE**

Carver met God in the secret place and had total faith, confidence, and peace that He would answer his questions. And He did. Carver explained that God told him to "separate the peanut into water, fats, oils, gums, resins, sugars, starches, and amino acids. Then recombine these under My three laws of compatibility, temperature, and pressure. Then, the Lord said, 'then you will know why I made the peanut!'"

Ten days later, George Washington Carver knew more than three hundred ways to put peanuts to work. That is the secret of the secret place—it isn't just a woo-woo, warm and fuzzy experience, it is a place of divine revelation. The Spirit of God is the most creative force in the universe because He's the Creator! And let me tell you friend, if He has a purpose for peanuts, He *definitely* has a purpose for you.

God brings solutions and creativity into this world, and He wants to do it through you. Now, I know some of you haven't felt His presence since you were a kid. Others of you might have never experienced it at all. But I promise, He's been relentless in His pursuit of you all along. And I've met God in the secret place praying for you to meet Him there too.

It's time to rekindle that relationship—or maybe even enter into it for the first time. I want to spend the rest of this chapter with my friend and pastor Ashli Van Horn. She's going to guide us through a special way of meeting God in the secret place through Sozo prayer. She's guided hundreds of people through this experience, and I invite you to join us.

SOZO PRAYER

Some of us are living on yesterday's bread! We're holding on to moldy manna and need a fresh experience with Him. Did you know there is more for you in the secret place than inspiration or getting your marching orders? There is incredible healing for your entire person as well.

Sozo prayer is an inner healing ministry pioneered by Bethel* that

SCAN ME

[*] **LEARN MORE ABOUT SOZO PRAYER HERE**

SCAN ME

^{**} **CONNECT WITH ASHLI, CHECK OUT HER BOOKS, AND LEARN MORE ABOUT HER MINISTRY HERE**

Ashli^{**} has trained in. Its main goal is to eliminate any barriers between you and the Father, Son, and Holy Spirit. And your connection to the Trinity is where the secret place is. Most often, those barriers are what prevent our healing too.

I experienced Sozo prayer for the first time when I was twenty-five, after family week at an addiction recovery center. Just like the empowerment triangle we talked about in chapter 7, Sozo prayer helped me break free from negative spiritual cycles. I realized I was carrying a backpack full of hurt, sorrow, and unforgiveness. But until then, I didn't realize those experiences constantly weighed me down. Imagine living saddled with a backpack full of rocks. You'd be carrying unnecessary weight with every step. But the sneaky part about unforgiveness is that it makes you think the weight is justified.

I had every natural reason to maintain that offense. But I learned forgiveness is something I *wanted* to do because it set me free. I took off that backpack of burdens and felt light for the first time in years. Sozo helps us continue this process by releasing judgment and punishment into God's hands. This unties us from the offenses.

This inner healing comes through forgiveness, both experiencing God's forgiveness to us and then extending that same forgiveness to others. The most toxic substance on earth isn't a virus or nuclear waste—it is unforgiveness. Sozo is a method of releasing trauma and pain in God's presence. We take time to work them out in the hidden places in our hearts, and God heals us, restoring what's been broken.

It's easy to make the secret place big, abstract, and far away when it's actually right beside us. God wants to meet us. And better yet, He knows how to speak to us exactly how we're created! For some of us, it's especially in nature. For others of us, it's in a favorite coffee shop in the morning. Wherever and whenever, God is there. But sometimes we don't slow down enough to recognize when God is speaking and moving. Life is rushed and we miss so many signposts pointing to what He's up to in our lives.

We can make a habit to catch these moments by pausing to ask two simple questions:

1. God, are you talking to me?
2. What would you like to say to me?

Lean into these conversations. In one of her books, Ashli explains listening to God like this. Imagine you're talking to someone with a really thick accent, where you need to focus and listen hard. You need to slow down to understand them. These are the training wheels to hearing God and recognizing His voice. When you ask God something, there are three sources of information: God, yourself, and the enemy (who can also mimic your voice, or even God's).

So how do we know who the heck is talking?

There was a man named Job in the Old Testament (there's a whole book written about his story). He was a good man with abundant wealth and a wonderful life. Honestly, his world was nothing but parties and trips to cash checks at the bank until one day, massive tragedies struck. He lost everything—his wealth, his health, and even his family.

Job had a long conversation with some friends. They were wrestling with the question, "Why did all of this get taken from you?" Job's friends had opinions. Job had opinions. And the enemy was the one who tried to take Job down in the first place. But eventually, Job asked, "Does not the ear test words as the tongue tastes food?" (Job 12:11).

Have you ever played the game where you eat blindfolded and try to guess what you're tasting? You know what strawberries, chocolate, and peanut butter taste like, so you can name the food. This was what Job was describing, only it was about hearing God's voice. He was saying our ears need to have a palate for God's voice. There's a lot of noise, many different tastes floating around, and we need to learn, over and over, what God's voice sounds like.

To do this, we simply keep going back to God. And Sozo prayer is a perfect place to start. You can even start on your own. Here's how to approach it.

1. Create a quiet, uninterrupted space in a place where you know you experience God. This may be in your basement, driving, listening to music, or hiking in nature.

2. When you pray, believe that the Lord meets you and hears you. He loves to show up for His kids. He can't wait for us to start talking to Him. He's just always talking and hardwired us with the capacity to hear from Him.

3. If you're asking God a question, it's good to respond to your knee-jerk reaction. What's the first thing you hear? God will partner with you in a conversation with Him to understand the information you hear. There are three sources of information: you, God, and the enemy. God's voice will always be redemptive, with His correction smothered in grace. His heart is for us to be

close. The enemy's greatest victory is when he speaks lies and we hear them in our own voice, internalizing them. The Holy Spirit will help you discern the source of information.

If you feel stuck, apply grace to yourself and continue the dialogue. Remember Jesus's words in Matthew 7:7, "Ask and it will be given to you; seek and you will find; knock and the door will be opened to you." Keep seeking. Keep knocking. God will open the door. We all hear from God differently—so my Sozo will be different than yours. There are thinkers, feelers, seers, and knowers. I am an extremely visual person, usually seeing pictures of what God is saying to me. These are all valid forms of communication!*

SCAN ME

* MY FRIEND AND BRILLIANT BIBLE TEACHER HAVILAH CUNNINGTON HAS A FREE QUIZ THAT HELPS YOU UNCOVER HOW YOU HEAR FROM GOD MOST CLEARLY

Begin your Sozo session with three questions (I've also included an example from a friend's Sozo session of what you may experience).

1. **God, who do I need to forgive?**

   Forgiveness means letting go of an offense. We extend the same forgiveness to others that God has given to us. Forgiveness opens up the secret place.

   Example: "Forgive your mom for not being there for you when you needed her."

2. **What lie am I believing because of that situation or offense?**

   Forgive them, then reject and abandon the lies you have believed because of this unforgiveness.

   Example: "I am believing that I'm not good enough for my mom to care about me. I don't believe I'm worth her time or attention, and I feel so lonely.

3. **If I give you these lies, what truth do you want to give me?**
   God makes good exchanges—we give God a terrible mess and He redeems it by replacing lies with the truth.
   Example: "God, I give you the lie that I'm not good enough for my mom. I forgive her for not being there for me when I really needed her. I accept the truth that I am loved, worthy, and Your daughter."

My friend, your secret place is a safe place God has prepared for you. It isn't scary or imaginary—we were made to be with God. Your body cries out on a molecular level for this closeness! These questions are simple but also transformative. Beginning with forgiveness might surprise you, but it is truly the gateway to the secret place. After all, we are able to boldly approach God's throne because we are forgiven in Jesus! Forgiveness will always be the pathway to healing and wholeness.

Lord, teach us to pray!

No matter if you've been seeking the secret place for forty minutes or forty years, please know it's okay if you don't feel like you truly know how to pray. Remember, the disciples spent all day every day with Jesus, and they still wanted to know how to pray like He did when they watched Him in His secret place. They asked, "Lord, teach us to pray . . ." (Luke 11:1).

Your meeting place with God will look different than mine. But you can start going to deep places with God right now. You can experience His power. You can be filled with supernatural energy to do the amazing things He has planned for you. There is great destiny on your life! But just like David, we need to spend time alone with God in the field before facing off against giants in the Valley of Elah.

The secret place is for now. It's available to you. Slow down and meet the Creator of the Universe there!

SCAN ME

" I INVITE YOU TO LISTEN TO
IN THE GARDEN BY STEPH ALESSI MUINA ON
SPOTIFY

In the Garden

I'll never forget that moment

My persistent heart was broken

My future out of focus

This faithful soul almost hopeless

Lifted by hands of devotion

And he walks with me, and he talks with me

And tells me I am his own

And the joy we share, As we tarry there

None other has ever known

I was out of breath from chasing

Chasing a world that was fading

I lost all my hope in the waiting

Lifted by hands of devotion

When the load is heavy

And when the day is long

When my strength is failing

I know right where you are

Mark 16:15

"He said to them, 'Go into all the world and preach the Good News to everyone." (NLT)

CHAPTER 17

THE SIGNIFICANT SUMMER

If you could spend three months with your family doing anything, what would you choose?

Would you travel the world?

Would you retreat deep into the mountains?

Would you stay home and just *be*?

Doug and I have been blessed to spend significant time doing all these things with our kids. But about one month after we launched Doug's book, *Church Boy to Millionaire*, we took our family, a film crew, and a jack-of-all-trades team across the country. We could have done many different things in those three months. But for some crazy reason, we set off on a ninety-eight-day, twenty-five-city tour of the United States called Massive Momentum. We believed we had a message to share that was going to help thousands of families create momentum in their lives. But we had no idea what, or who, it would take to pull it off.*

In fact, we didn't even know what it was going to look like. When we began talking about making some tour stops, people asked us to explain what the events were going to be about.

Was Massive Momentum going to be a bunch of health events? No.

·1 FAMILY·

·98 DAYS·

·25 CITIES·

·1000's EMPOWERED·

STARTING is not most people's problem, FINISHING IS.

MASSIVE MOMENTUM

EMPOWERING PEOPLE TO LIVE ON PURPOSE

AN ORIGINAL DOCUMENTARY

SCAN ME

· YOU CAN WATCH THE FULL DOCUMENTARY HERE

Was it going to be a series of church events? No.

So, what was it going to be? Until we took the stage on opening night in Phoenix, we honestly didn't know. All we knew was who it was for: anyone looking for a breakthrough in life.

We had no idea what God had in store for us. The impactful nights and changed lives continue to amaze us. But the journey in between cities, beautiful venues, and bright stage lights wasn't so glamorous. It was one of the most significant summers my family has ever spent together. It changed us forever. The Massive Momentum tour helped transform hundreds of people's lives; it also transformed ours.

It started out, like so many things, as a fun idea for Doug to share his heart behind the book in a few different cities. But the invitations to come speak kept rolling in and Doug's calendar filled up. I saw all the dates and realized this wasn't something for him to fly solo, we needed to join him as a family. Because even together, the road can still be a lonely place.

We were initially going to buy a sprinter van. They're sleek, efficient, and perfect for the grind of loading gear in and out. But they're not so perfect for three kids and two adults! Can you imagine living in a sardine can like that with a two-year-old boy? Three and a half months with five people wasn't going to happen.

We purchased an RV, a trailer, and even a Jeep Wrangler to pull behind it. Had it wrapped. And with life-sized pictures of Doug and I on the RV, we hit the road. We stuck out everywhere we went, pulling into little towns and big cities, winding through crowded streets, praying our GPS was taking us to the right destination. A caravan of people ready to kick fear in the face!

But none of us thought it would be that hard until the middle. You know, after we'd been away for over a month and we got a little homesick. It turned out that fear kicked us in the face hard from Day One.

Our first event was in Phoenix, right at our front door. People should stream in, right? We'd booked a venue that could pack hundreds of

MASSIVE MOMENTUM

EMPOWERING PEOPLE TO LIVE ON PURPOSE

tour dates

MAY 3RD PHOENIX, AZ

MAY 10TH SAN DIEGO, CA

MAY 11TH ANAHEIM, CA

MAY 16TH BAY AREA, CA

MAY 17TH SACRAMENTO, CA

MAY 23RD SALEM, OR

MAY 24TH PORTLAND, OR

MAY 28TH BOISE, ID

MAY 31ST SALT LAKE CITY, UT

JUNE 3RD DENVER, CO

JUNE 6TH TULSA, OK

JUNE 8TH BENTONVILLE, AR

JUNE 10TH DALLAS, TX

JUNE 14TH TUSCALOOSA, AL

JUNE 18TH NASHVILLE, TN

JUNE 20TH INDIANAPOLIS, IN

JUNE 22ND ROCKFORD, IL

JUNE 27TH LEXINGTON, KY

JUNE 28TH CINCINNATI, OH

JUNE 29TH CLEVELAND, OH

JULY 7TH BROOKLYN, NY

JULY 10TH WASHINGTON, DC

JULY 12TH BALTIMORE, MD

JULY 18TH CHARLESTON, SC

AUGUST 1ST TAMPA, FL

people. The only problem was that we'd sold barely 10 percent of the tickets by the morning of the event. And already, it seemed like our massive tour was going to be massively underwhelming. We were excited to share a message of momentum and liberation to anyone who would listen, but some anxiety surfaced that first night.

Still, we showed up at the venue—a large church building in Scottsdale. This was also the first time we really got a handle on how much gear we were about to be hauling across the country. Doug had a clothing line, The Real Doug Wood. I, of course, had the Kick Fear in the Face line. Add to that thousands of copies of *Church Boy to Millionaire*, and we were filled to the brim with merchandise.

Over the next three months we would transform lobbies, foyers, and even airport hangars into pop-up shops—with hoodies, shirts, bomber jackets, snapback hats, and of course, books! Thankfully that first night, people swarmed the event, buying tickets at the door. We opened the tour to a couple hundred people hungry for breakthrough in their lives.

There was no turning back now. We took pictures, signed books, said our goodbyes, and then got busy tearing everything down to do it all over again in a couple of days in San Diego, the start of our West Coast leg. Here we go.

PEEK BEHIND THE SCENES OF THE SET UP

WHEN YOU WANT TO QUIT

We weren't even three stops in and we wanted to quit. The people were amazing—but life on the road was grueling. Already, the miles, the setup and teardown, and lack of space made our skin crawl. Then we pulled into San Francisco and got a dose of how wild things could really get.

Silicon Valley is one of the most expensive areas in the whole country. Finding the right venue with a place for our crew was a challenge. But we finally secured a venue at what we thought was a nicer hotel. It was in a pocket of the city that looked fine on the internet. But looks can be deceiving, especially on a screen. Let's just say it wasn't what we expected.

The hotel was old school and had the vibe that people rented rooms by the hour. The issue was that it wasn't just for an event, our team was staying here. We helped them check in then decided to find some food. Everything was going to be better after a meal, we thought.

We towed a red Jeep Wrangler behind our RV, and our videographers, Jeff and Ashlyn, drove our black Escalade. We all piled in, ate some great Mexican food, and then went back to the hotel to get the team settled before finding an RV park for our family to stay for the night. We returned to a problem—a very smelly one.

The RV reeked of sewage, like a pipe had burst. It was unbearable. Doug covered his

PHOENIX, AZ

SAN DIEGO, CA

FULLERTON, CA

nose and stepped into the RV of doom to find the source. Fortunately, he didn't find any leaky sewage water. Instead, he found that the gas stove had been running. Easy fix! He reached down to turn off the gas—only instead of cutting the gas, he accidentally pressed the igniter.

Whoosh!

I kid you not, flames instantly burst out onto Doug's arm, singeing off his hair and burning him. Thank goodness the mini explosion didn't blow up the RV. After turning off the gas and checking Doug's arm for third-degree burns, we were finally ready to wind down for the night and sleep. It was well after 10 p.m. at this point, and we'd already driven five hundred miles from San Diego that day.

nothing to see here

We wound through the curving streets of San Francisco in our wrapped RV, just barely squeaking through some tight spots to finally pull into the RV park. Only it wasn't a campground like we expected—it was a mobile home park where people actually lived! The surrounding area was also extremely shady. And of course we were driving a vehicle with a giant Doug and Thea on the side. I felt like we stuck out enough to be seen from space.

It was 11 p.m. at that point and we had to track down the office to find our parking spot. When we finally pulled in for the night though, instead of relief, Doug and I felt terrible. We knew we were not in a safe place. And not only were our kids with us, but our team was back in a questionable hotel situation as well.

Our responsibility to our team and our kids weighed heavily on us. We'd put everyone in danger and felt like we were in way over our heads. Maybe we shouldn't have jumped into the deep end of the pool, after all.

Doug slept with his gun under his pillow that night. He woke up at 5 a.m. the next morning, walked to get us coffee, and kept wondering what on earth we were thinking. After the San Francisco event, we headed north to Sacramento for the fifth Massive Momentum night. Guess what?

The next morning when we were hopping in the vehicles to go, we saw glass all over the ground around the Escalade. It had been broken into during the night! So here we were, only four stops in. We'd almost blown up the RV, Doug slept with a gun under his pillow, and we'd been robbed.

Yep—we wanted to quit. With twenty-one events to go, nearly all the fight had already been knocked out of us. But we gritted our teeth and headed north to Portland. We were going home and praying for an amazing night the entire drive up.

SAN FRANCISCO, CA

SACRAMENTO, CA

FULL CIRCLE

Have you ever had a full-circle moment? When you return to a significant place in your life but you're a different person than before? That was Portland. The city hadn't changed, but we had.

We held our event in the annex at the Rose Garden, packing about four hundred people in. The aromatic smell of flowers filled the air, with roses of every color popping brilliantly against the deep Oregon greenery. Doug's friends from high school, family, church friends, and new friends all mingled. Old and new swirled together in a truly beautiful evening. Amaya, fourteen at the time, spoke and brought the house down—with many of her friends in the audience!* It was even Katelyn's birthday.

The hometown crew showed up for a powerful night and put some

SCAN ME

 WATCH AMAYA'S TALK HERE

AMAYA, ME, AND OUR FRIEND JENNY QUIRIE ON THE PORTLAND STOP

wind in our sails. San Francisco and Sacramento had shown us that we were far deeper in than we thought. But Portland reminded us of the people whose lives had changed alongside ours. Later in the tour, I would fly back to Portland for a wedding and have coffee with a friend who'd been with us that night.

She told me that no matter how I was feeling, she knew God was laying major groundwork for what he wanted to do through our family—and all the families that joined us along the way. My friend had no idea how badly Doug and I had wanted to pack up and limp home. Our reality wasn't turning out anything like our dream. The tour was ten times harder than we'd imagined it would be. But what do you do when you show up for your dream and it turns out to be nothing like you thought?

You ask yourself whether it's worth it. We knew it was. A life of significance isn't easy. In fact, it's almost guaranteed not to be. Doing significant things is really hard. But at every stop, we met dozens of people who were doing hard things alongside us.

They were contending for marriages, health, their children, their finances, their faith, and even their lives. From Portland, we headed east toward Idaho, knowing that at least one person needed some life breathed into them. That was enough to make our discomfort worth it.

SALEM, OR

PORTLAND, OR

BREAKING FALLOW GROUND

The event in Boise, Idaho was one of the smallest on the tour. The venue was pretty standard—but the community was electric! The morning of the event, I woke up early for a walk to a local coffee shop and invited anyone who'd like to join me. I pulled on my Community Starter T-shirt and got moving. Over thirty people showed up at the coffee shop!

This immediately told me that the people in this city were hungry for transformation. They were willing to show up to spark massive momentum in their lives, families, and community!

That night, I said to the eighty people who came, "I know there are eighty of you out there, but I feel like I'm speaking to thousands of people. You're bringing the energy of a packed stadium! There is power in this room. Your stories matter."

Then I was flat-out honest with them.

"We almost wanted to call this whole thing off. It was already getting too hard. But tonight breathed a lot of hope into us!"

Our souls needed this. We knew that it didn't matter if there were four hundred people in the room or forty, God called us to go. So we would keep going.

The first leg of the tour felt like going for a hard run without warming up. Our joints were stiff. Our shoes didn't fit right. Our laces kept coming untied. And everything in us wanted to walk back home, shut the curtains, turn on Netflix, and try again later. It felt like we were breaking fallow ground.

Fallow ground is soil that's been left without anything planted in it. It's just sitting there beneath the sun, rain, and snow. It has the potential to yield life, but there are no seeds. As a farm girl I saw fallow fields dotting the landscape every year. Some fields are allowed to rest so that their nutrients can return and the soil will be more fruitful.

During this time though, the ground gets hard. Tumbleweeds

BOISE, ID

bounce and skip across weeds and empty earth. When it's time to plant again, that fallow ground needs to be broken. And it's a lot of work!

I realize now that while we were traveling to help others find breakthroughs, God was doing something new in us. The never-ending hustle and grind wore us thin. But something broke in Boise. Like the top layer of hardened mud cracking open, unearthing rich black soil, filled with nutrients, ready for new seed.

What fallow ground is God trying to break in your heart right now? Where have weeds crept in? What potential in you has laid unplanted for too long? Where has your soil become overrun with thorns? Where has your spirit gotten hard? Where has bitterness taken root? Where has despair buried itself like dead fence posts?

God wants to break your fallow ground—and He's going to use hard things to break your hardness. I know firsthand. It hurts, but it clears the way for abundant life.

I believe that the days we don't feel like showing up are the most important. Because it's those days that separate the doers from the dreamers. Those are the days we kick fear in the face and follow through on our commitments. Those are the days we see what we're really made of—and God does His finest work in us *and* through us.

NO ACCIDENTS

We carried that energy with us from Boise to Birmingham. We traveled further south to Tuscaloosa, Alabama and connected with more amazing people. Scott and Kristi Schatzline are the pastors of Daystar Church in Tuscaloosa, and God had already been using them in a special way in our lives. They're the kind of people you instantly connect with when you first meet them. Our daughters, Amaya and Destiny, even became best friends.

Scott and Kristi had ushered a new season of worship into our lives, and the week we spent there was a continuation of that. We needed

SALT LAKE CITY, UT

DENVER, CO

TULSA, OK

some refreshing and we found it! Honestly, we've never been served and taken care of like we were in Tuscaloosa. They knew we were hungry or thirsty before we did. When you get around people like this, they call you to a higher realm of servant leadership.

This stop powered us up for our trip north and eventually to the East Coast leg. Our family was excited because after several more tour stops, we were going to spend one week of family vacation in the Hamptons in New York. It's a beautiful area where the grassy hills give way to perfect beaches, with houses lined along the seashore. It was supposed to be total rest and family fun—only the week was invaded by another massive commitment Doug and I had made. We spent our time in the beautiful Hamptons planning and strategizing a three-thousand-person conference we were co-hosting in the fall.

From 5 a.m. to 10 p.m. we lived on Zoom scratching out schedules, potential speakers, and logistical needs for hosting so many people. And from here, we threw ourselves back into the cycle of setup, tear down, repeat—all the way from New York to Florida.

At the end of the East Coast leg we went to a separate convention in Orlando where hundreds of Massive Momentum folks attended. It was overwhelming and beautiful. So many people swarmed us and said they'd leveled up, hired parenting coaches, and done so many positive things to get momentum in their lives. We saw fruit. There is nothing quite as magical as seeing fruit hang from the branches of a tree you worked hard to plant and nurture.

We also were empowered by a worship song the amazingly talented artist Steph Alessi Muina wrote and performed called "Echo". Her words reminded us that not only were we making an eternal impact—but we were never alone in our work, regardless of how hard things would get.

BENTONVILLE, AR

DALLAS, TX

TUSCALOOSA, AL

NASHVILLE, TN

INDIANAPOLIS, IN

Echo

My ears are filled with songs of destiny

My faith goes as far as my eyes can see

The path that was once a mystery

Has been brightened by a voice calling me

I hear the echo of my purpose calling me

I'm not afraid

Wherever, wherever I go

You are with me, You are with me

Wherever, wherever I go

You are with me, You are with me

Clearer now than ever I can see

Your plans for me are more than I could dream

I'm running after you with everything

You're calling out to me, I'm listening

I hear the echo of my purpose

Calling me

SCAN ME

· LISTEN TO ECHO BY STEPH ALESSI MUINA

We learned that so many thought they were the only ones dealing with heartache, addiction, or fear. Thousands of people from one coast to the other shared so much more than they ever thought. These were powerful moments because not only did people feel seen and heard, they felt connected to a community so much bigger than themselves.

Our event in Atlanta was the perfect example.

Until this event, Doug and I had been intentional about not trying to push our faith onto others. If they wanted to talk about Jesus or spirituality, we were all about it. But we wanted to respect every stage of life and group of people, no matter where they stood spiritually. That night in Atlanta, though, the energy was different. A feeling of significance, destiny, and power filled the room before any of the people arrived.

Most nights, at the end of our talks, we opened up a microphone for questions or testimonies. This night, a woman stood up and opened her heart to the whole crowd.

"This is the last event my husband and I were ever going to attend as a couple. We had agreed to divorce after this. But after hearing from you tonight, we are recommitting to our marriage."

The audience burst into applause as tears streamed down her cheeks. And then a teenage boy stood to proclaim that he was taking authority over his pornography addiction. One after the other, people stood declaring life in some places that had been fallow for a long time.

Then one last woman stood, and it was like I had a direct download from God just for her. I told her, "You're worth it. You're a child of God. You have a purpose and a destiny that is much greater than you can see. You are going to find victory over the alcoholism that's been robbing you of your breakthrough!"

I knew she wasn't there by accident, and I felt God's overwhelming love for her, which was so massive it was like trying to hold back an ocean tide.

It was such a powerful experience I felt like if this was the only woman I reached all tour, it would've still been worth it. That's what

CHICAGO, IL

LEXINGTON, KY

CINCINNATI, OH

CLEVELAND, OH

BROOKLYN, NY

WASHINGTON DC

ATLANTA, GA

TAMPA, FL

NEW ORLEANS, LA

SAN ANTONIO, TX

happens when you focus on the one, the person God has placed right in front of you. The man, woman, or kiddo that you can love and serve. All the vehicle breakdowns and break-ins, the fires and discouragements, every one of them was worth it.

And isn't that what significance is? It's about investing your life into something that is worth the blood, sweat, tears, and RV fires. These events were genuinely significant for those who attended. But they were far more significant for our family than I had imagined.

We watched our girls rise up. All summer long Katelyn ran the book table and helped sell over a thousand books. Amaya managed tens of thousands of dollars in merchandise. Our girls were our rocks, and we seriously couldn't have done it without them. The entire summer felt like a wild carnival, like the ones I used to help my grandparents with. My girls got a taste of carney life and absolutely blossomed. Did some hard things come with ninety-eight unpredictable days on the road? Sure. But the Wood girls learned they can do hard things in service to others.

I am reminded of this every Sunday as my girls serve as baristas at our church coffee shop. It's significant because we converted our Massive Momentum trailer into the coffee shop itself! That trailer traveled across the country serving people. Let me tell you, if God can use a trailer, He can use you! Just like He's using my beautiful girls.

Friend, what is the significant season it's time for you to step into? Are you holding back from it? Are you dancing around the edge listening to the whispers of fear and doubt? Are you staring at the deep end of the pool wondering if you'll be able to stay afloat?

Here is my best advice: if God has called you, jump.

What is God asking you to do? Does it seem crazy big? If it seems too crazy and too big and too scary, you're probably seeing it right. Will it be hard? Absolutely. But more important is the answer to this question: will it be worth it?

Doug and I have a saying: the answer to "how?" is always "yes." Action diffuses fear. And if God has called you to show up, He's faithful to show you how. Our significant summer was hard—but the rewards weren't for us. Your significant season will be hard too—but the rewards aren't just for you, either.

YOUR LIFE MATTERS.

YOUR STORY MATTERS.

YOUR LEGACY MATTERS.

We need you to keep going. Chase the significance you were born for and remember that Fear Kickers don't have a quitter's bone in their bodies. The winners are the ones who just don't quit.

No matter where you are at on your journey, there are future generations who will say your name with gratitude because you did the hard things. They will cry tears of thanks when they learn how hard you contended for the blessings they enjoy. They will be in awe that your blood runs through their veins.

Your choice to kick fear in the face will give them strength to pick up where you leave off. Now go, partner with your future self, and step into your significant season.

family fun along the tour

ARK ENCOUNTER, KY

CRIMSON TIDE TOUR, AL

DISNEY

LAKE TUSCALOOSA, AL

NEW ORLEANS, LA

NEW YORK, NY

PLANTATION, SC

SUNDANCE, UT

SUNDANCE, UT

PHOENIX, AZ

SAN DIEGO, CA

FULLERTON, CA

PORTLAND, OR

BOISE, ID

SALT LAKE CITY, UT

DALLAS, TX

TUSCALOOSA, AL

INDIANAPOLIS, IN

CLEVELAND, OH

TARRYTOWN, NY

WASHINGTON DC

SAN FRANCISCO, CA

SACRAMENTO, CA

SALEM, OR

DENVER, CO

TULSA, OK

BENTONVILLE, AR

CHICAGO, IL

LEXINGTON, KY

CINCINNATI, OH

ATLANTA, GA

TAMPA, FL

NEW ORLEANS, LA

That's a wrap!

SAN ANTONIO, TX

SHOUT OUT TO THE MASSIVE MOMENTUM CREW!

THE RACE OF A LIFETIME

I had trained for the Jerusalem Marathon for months. On my training runs I imagined myself on the ancient streets where Jesus walked. This race had been a dream, and finally in March 2020, it was going to happen—until it was canceled because of the COVID-19 pandemic.

I was crushed when I heard the news. Preparing for a marathon isn't easy, but managing my disappointment was even harder. While I could have bowed out, I knew in my heart and spirit I needed to fulfill my commitment to myself, run this race on my own, and bring Jerusalem to Scottsdale.

Reflecting on this experience, I see that the journey of 26.2 miles is like so many others we take in life. No matter how many training miles you put in, you never quite feel prepared to leave that starting line. There is so much chatter in your head, little voices whispering, "You should have trained more . . . This is too hard . . . You don't have to do this . . . Everyone will understand if you quit . . ."

But on March 20, 2020, I silenced those whispers and ran my Jerusalem Marathon in Scottsdale. Mile by mile, it changed my life.

Mile 1. The starting line is always electric. You're pumped full of adrenaline and butterflies, and your nervous energy is dying to be released into the pavement. Your friends and family are there cheering you on, sharing their energy with you. You can see the finish line in your head and your only mission is to start strong and ease into the proper pace. It's go time!

Mile 3. The first two miles melt away your enthusiasm. Reality sets in. And you realize that even though you've run a 5K, you're barely 10 percent into this thing. Those little voices of doubt start to percolate. "What the heck did you get yourself into?!" Every breath comes a little harder, and that vision of the finish line is starting to get blurry.

Mile 5. After battling the doubt for a couple more miles, I see my house! My route takes me down the familiar desert roads crisscrossing through cacti and arid trails. My friends and family are gathered to cheer me on—it's all high fives and "Go girl!" Phoenix is waiting in his stroller, and I get to push him for about half a mile. I have over twenty miles left, but now I also have momentum. And momentum is invaluable. Just keep moving. Right, left . . . Right, left . . . Repeat.

Mile 8. Momentum is with me, but now it's key that I control my breathing, stay fueled, and keep hydrating. This is a pulse check. What I do now determines how the rest of the race will play out. Even though I was the only runner, I realized I was still in a competition against myself. My only job was to keep going. I was running a race with my mind, not just my body.

Mile 12. I am on top of the world! More people are strategically positioned to cheer me on. I know I can do this. My body feels light and I'm filled with the crazy energy of a runner's high. I feel unstoppable. My body and mind are in perfect alignment. I've got this!

Mile 18. Welcome to the *major* crash. I run alone for the next two miles, exhausted and in pain. My joints hurt, my feet ache, and I feel hollow, like I've sprung a leak and all that beautiful mile twelve energy drained away. The only person with me is my friend, Sumer Morenz, who rides her bike behind me the entire way. She knows I'm

SUMMER RIDING HER BIKE BEHIND ME

PASTOR ASHLI CHEERING ME ON

struggling and finds a couple of new songs to help me get my head back into the race.

Moments like this make you realize how important your beehive community is. When everyone is gone and you still have miles ahead, that one person can make all the difference. But these were the miles where I needed some real grit. No matter how encouraging Sumer was, she couldn't lace up my shoes and run the miles for me. This was my race and no one could put in the work for me.

These are the miles that show you what you're made of.

Mile 22. Doug reminds me of what's at the end. My children are waiting for me at a fountain surrounded by gorgeous horse statues—a little nod to my heritage. I want them to see their mom finish strong. These miles have shown me that the biggest reason I'd been training wasn't just to improve physically or even mentally, but spiritually. The hundreds of miles equaled hours spent with God in prayer and worship. They were filled with memories of my grandparents and a vision of who my children would become. And as I neared the fountain, a circular rainbow spun itself around the sun, bringing Hebrews 12:1 to life:

Therefore, since we are surrounded by such a great cloud of witnesses, let us throw off everything that hinders and the sin that so easily entangles. And let us run with perseverance the race marked out for us, fixing our eyes on Jesus, the pioneer and perfecter of faith.

The Finish Line. I was surrounded by my cloud of witnesses and ended my race in joyful tears. Feelings of massive accomplishment washed over me. I felt strength from all the generations before me and hope for all of those ahead.

This was the hardest thing I have ever done in my life—harder than birthing all three of my children! But it was also one of the most rewarding because I have a new deadly arrow in my confidence quiver: *I can freaking do hard things.* The voices of fear and doubt don't control me. My purpose does.

DOUG MY GREATEST CHEERLEADER AND COACH IN LIFE

RAINBOW AROUND THE SUN!

VICTORY!!!

CALLING MY MOM & SISTER

MY KIDS HOLDING THE FINISH LINE

IT WASN'T SUPPOSED
TO BE THIS WAY

I was *supposed* to be in Jerusalem. The world wasn't supposed to shut down. Have you ever felt this way? Wondering, how on earth did I end up here?!

I was *supposed* to have a better career . . .

I was *supposed* to be married to the perfect person . . ..

I was *supposed* to have children by now . . .

I was *supposed* to live in a different city . . .

I was *supposed* to be so much farther along . . .

You may be feeling like you're supposed to be in Jerusalem but somehow you got stuck in Scottsdale. But I believe that God had planned for me to run this race in the wrong place all along. Because it wasn't the earth I would run on that was magic, it was about who God would help me become along the way. I brought my Jerusalem dream to Scottsdale that day. You can do this too.

Fear Kicker, it's not about the *place*; it's about the *promise*. The promise God has made to never leave you or forsake you. To make you more than a conqueror. To write your name in the Book of Life. It's also about the promise you make to yourself, your family, and your community: I will not quit.

You were made for great things. It's time for you to run the race of a lifetime!

Find your voice. Nobody else has your story, and someone needs to hear it today.

Build your beehive community. We are better together. As the ancient proverb says, if you want to go fast, go alone. If you want to go far, go together.

Embrace structure. Structure determines your behavior. Ignite your Spark Habits to say your best yes every day.

Get outside. Connect with God in creation. Get grounded every day, walk the earth barefoot, and stand in awe of what God has made.

Let your spirit break out. Proclaim God's Word, promises, and power in every situation. His presence changes the atmosphere!

Bring them a lean and green. Serve your way to success. Love people where they are at. It's not about wanting things from people; it's wanting things for them.

Step outside of the drama zone. Live above drama, draw a do-not-cross line, and hold your ground like your life depends on it—because it does.

Accept generational blessings and break generational curses. There are wonderful things former generations have done for you. Gratefully accept those. But also remember you are a chain-breaker; set future generations free.

Kick it with Esther. What you do today matters—you are on earth for such a time as this!

Let shift happen. Trust that God's plan is actually better than yours. Shift happens; welcome the new and don't look back to the old.

Remember your victor's crown. Worship is a weapon—use it daily and walk in victory.

Love Jesus (and cuss a little). Get angry at the evil trying to take us out and stand against it with everything you've got.

Slay like David. You were born to slay giants. Your days spent with God in the field choking out lions and killing bears are preparing you for the battle of a lifetime.

Pick up your shield. Put on the full armor of God daily, stand strong against the enemy of our souls, and get into action when God calls out your name!

Find your secret place. Keep seeking, knocking, and meeting God in the secret place He has prepared just for you.

Live with significance. Your significant season will be hard—but it isn't just for you. Thousands are counting on you to show up and keep running. Your yes is their breakthrough.

Kick fear in the face! Now, it's your turn to run. Grab the baton, kick fear in the face, and shine bright in this world!

ABOUT THE AUTHOR

Doug and Thea Wood are entrepreneurs who run a multi-million dollar independent coaching business. Over the last nine years, they have helped over 300,000 people improve their lives. They've dedicated their lives to helping average people (just like them) with above average desires to live and become their best selves.

They imagine a world where people live and express the riches within, rather than purely pursue the riches without. Doug and Thea's authentic and relatable communication style creates instant connections with anyone who desires more for their life. They are in demand speakers and the co-founders of Valor Global Online, an innovative school bringing synergy to students and their families worldwide.

They have also been called the entrepreneur family, as their three children, Amaya (18), Katelyn (15), and Phoenix (6), are also writing books, speaking, starting businesses of their own, and fully embracing their family's legacy.

Most importantly, the Wood family has chosen to live life differently, set apart from average. When they're not traveling the world, they live in Scottsdale, Arizona at their property, Breakthrough Acres.

ABOUT KICK FEAR
IN THE FACE

In 2011, when Kick Fear in the Face began, I was a captive to fear. I was locked up by what people thought of me. By feelings of inadequacy. And by total doubt in myself. Then, one day, this mantra came to me: Kick Fear In The Face. And I felt God whisper, "I see you. I know you. If you partner with Me and fully lean in, we can do this together."

It all started with this; a resolution that fear is a liar. The belief that we each have the potential for greatness. And about twenty tank-tops and hats! Then, in just a couple of days, the tanks and hats were being worn by my first fellow Fear Kickers. And every one of us embraced this lifestyle of living life out loud, and lives started to change—my own included.

Since those early days, the transformation stories have taught me something profound: our place of pain can become our power to reign. When we focus on our fear, we see only our obstacles. Our impact and potential is so limited. But when we see past it, beyond our tiny horizon, the sky opens up and we see what we can truly become. We see the lives we can impact—from our families to our cities to our world.

Kick Fear in the Face is a movement built on this core belief: our greatest potential is on the other side of fear! We each have a purpose, a God-sized plan for our lives. As a community, we're passionately proving this truth by the thousands. Every day, we choose to armor up, push past fear, and be way-makers, chain-breakers, and movement-makers in this world. With intentionality we choose to face fear head on to fulfill our God given destiny and purpose on this planet by providing people with resources and community to live life out loud. We empower through a community that speaks truth and life into one another!

Connect with us at: kickfearintheface.com
www.facebook.com/kickfearintheface

SHOUT OUTS

TO MY PARENTS

Thank you for being chain-breakers and way-makers! Thank you for teaching me to work hard and pray harder. And most of all, thank you for building our family upon the Rock of our Salvation, Jesus!

I will always treasure our whirlwind trip to visit Magnolia in Waco, Texas. It was two days of heaven on earth. Being with you reminded me how many millions of lives will come into the Kingdom because of your yes to follow Jesus. Thank you for showing the way to dwell in the house of the Lord forever.

A TRIP WITH MY PARENTS TO MAGNOLIA!

TO MY BEAUTIFUL SISTERS

I proclaim blessing over your children and future grandchildren! Your fingerprints are present in everything Kick Fear in the Face has become, and your partnership helped bring this movement into reality. From Mandy building the first website in 2016, to Misty pioneering our popup shops, to Tessa being the most beautiful model ever... THANK YOU!

Your sisterhood, many contributions, and partnership have been pivotal to bringing this fear-kicking movement, and this book, to life.

TO MY PARENTS-IN-LOVE

To Rick and Jeannette, my parents-in-love! You have embraced me as your daughter from Day One. Even though life has thrown lots of obstacles your way, you have risen above them, showing up consistently for your grandkids, Amaya, Katelyn, and Phoenix. They will always remember your dedication and the way you make them feel.

Jeanette, thank you for staying with the kids when we travel, and making them feel safe and always loved—they adore you! Rick, thank you for the many early airport runs and answering last-minute calls to shuttle the kids to all of their activities! Your grandkids love their time with you. Thank you!

TO MY SISTER-IN-LOVE

Jen, you have always managed to challenge and encourage me at the same time! Your talents blow me away—and you have used them to help bring some of my greatest dreams into reality. From small gatherings to large conferences, you've been the key ingredient to bring visions to life. I love you, and my beautiful nieces you birthed into this world, so much—what a legacy you have in Madelyn and Kenzie! And I love you because you choose to do hard things.

TO OUR SUPPORT TEAM

Alisha, you are an angel God sent into our lives! Thank you for tirelessly loving and helping our family. We could not accomplish God's mission for the Woods without you! Shay, thank you for coming alongside me for the first two years of Phoenix's life. Our divine partnership will have eternal impact! And Roxanne Hickman, thank you for all you do every day to keep our family organized! You are truly one in a million. Your love, support, and organization make our dreams a reality!

TO MY SCRIBE

In collaboration with my editor and scribe Jordan Loftis. Thanks for being my co-laborer in bringing this wisdom into the world for generations to come.

TO MY BOOK CREW

This book is one of the hardest things I've ever done—but we do hard things! And I could never have done it without my amazing book crew: Britt Rayburn, my designer extraordinaire who worked tirelessly to bring this beautiful book to life, Carlee Jean Richardson, my incredible photographer, Anna Thompson, the glue keeping everyone together, and Ashton Hauff, for additional design support. Thank you for helping me share this journey of kicking fear in the face!

TO OUR MASSIVE MOMENTUM TOUR CREW

A huge thank you to our Massive Momentum tour crew! Jeff and Ashlyn Rogers with Spin-Town Creative, thank you for capturing the experience on video and producing the documentary. Kari Rose and Carly O'Keeffe, you kept our beautiful books and clothing in stock at every stop. Shay Galloway and Misty Mann, you were godsends, jumping in at multiple stages when we needed extra hands. Our beautiful daughters, Amaya and Katelyn, you seriously rose to the occasion, running registration for thousands and our pop-up shops—plus helping with the endless set up and tear down. We do hard things as a family. Britt Rayburn, thank you for designing all of our social media marketing and Kick Fear Gear. Larae Siligia, your branding and design work on stage backdrops perfectly set the tone—especially the RV wrap (with the massive pictures of Doug and I on the side)! And thank you to our drivers, Rohmon Merchant and Daniel Drainer, for keeping us safe for so many miles on the road. Friends, your work impacted thousands of lives forever. Thank you for your partnership!

TO MY 17-WEEK WARRIORS

Every season brings new opportunities to grow, learn, expand, and build community. For me, community is always where breakthrough happens because it brings hope, vision, and fresh faith!

A few years ago, I was in a frustrating season where I needed a tangible sign from God. I knew He was there—but I desperately needed to see His hand guiding me. And He showed up in the most surprising, random way.

I began to see the number: 7:17. Morning and evening, I would see it in our house or in my car—always right at the exact time of 7:17. It took me a few days to realize it wasn't a coincidence. So I asked God, "What are You trying to tell me?"

I immediately went into research mode and discovered the Hebrew meaning of seven: the number of completeness, and physical and spiritual perfection. God created the universe in six days, calling it "very good." Then, He rested in the perfection of His creation on the seventh.

Next I learned the Hebrew meaning of seventeen symbolizes "complete victory" and "overcoming the enemy."

Then, I went a step further, combining these powerful numbers and found 717 means "to gather or pluck." And of course gathering means bringing together from scattered places, pluck can mean quickly removing someone from a dangerous situation!

This daily sign of 717 was a God wink reminding me that He has gathered fellow overcomers into my life, perfect for this season, and running hip-to-hip with me toward victory!

These women were my 17-week tribe! For 17 weeks, we gathered before I went into the writing sessions for Kick Fear in the Face. We prayed, worshiped, and encouraged each other—which gave me so much strength and focus to lay out my life's journey in the pages of this book.

Thank you: Jenny Cantu, Joyce Brown, Jaelyn Harrel, Shay Galloway, Tori Kruse, Kelsey Altringer, and Olivia Arellano for running with me! Thank you for challenging me, and one another, to make bold moves in the middle of a pandemic over Zooms and FaceTimes!

Seven of us joining together for seventeen weeks was a beautiful thing. God is faithful to always bring complete victory and breakthrough in our lives, and you were a part of that for me.

KICK FEAR EVENTS
OVER THE YEARS

Thank you to Karisa and Sumer for being some of the first Kick Fear in the Face models. Also, thank you to the many friends, pastors, and connections that have invited Kick Fear in the Face to be a part of your event, conference, or retreat. Fear Kickers are rising up across the globe because you have created the space for breakthrough!

KICK FEAR IN THE FACE!®